THRUMS

Odds and Ends for Handweavers and Dyers

by

Faithe Shaw Nunneley

Flower Valley Press

Rockville, Maryland

Illustrations by Leslie Burgess

Photographs by Seymour Bress

Cover photography by Lee Owens

ISBN - 0-9620543-3-X

Photos

Page iv. Jacket by Beverly Ryan. Eight-harness reverse twill; silk warp, weft rayon/cotton blend.

Page vii. Closeup of pattern motif on reversible room divider; brown and white linen. See page 111.

Page 1. "Friendship" vest in wool twill. Alternating gray and white squares embroidered by friends in a clothing study group.

Page 3. Vest in rya knots, machine-washable wool.

Page 7. Backstrap-woven band from Ecuador. Warp face, tightly spun alpaca; red, black, white, yellow and green.

Page 21. Two-block Summer and Winter weave. Warp and tabby 10/2 black cotton, pattern doubled floss in blue and green.

Page 35. Top in cotton warp with bouclé weft, supplementary warp pattern in cotton floss.

Page 41. Color wheel in Color Aid paper on black 28" x 44" mat board.

Page 47. "Minnesota Castles II" – silk inlay on cotton, 10" x 19".

Page 53. Bias top by Beverly Ryan; cannelé weave in silk, rayon and cotton.

Page 57. Detail of photo on page 89.

Page 65. Dyeing record of a value reduction.

Page 69. Four-block, six-harness Summer and Winter weave. Lower pattern in regular weave, upper pattern in Swivel weave with pattern floats on reverse.

Page 79. Italian Diamond (doubled Rose Path) pattern. White silk overshot and border woven against a plain black background of black silk; six harness for pattern and a pickup stick for border.

Page 85. Workshop sample in eight-harness double weave; various combinations of green, lavender, purple and blue (see page 89).

Page 89. Four block, six-harness Summer and Winter weave, showing use of isolated blocks on a standard Summer and Winter background.

Page 93. Back view of jacket by Beverly Ryan, shown on page iv.

Page 97. Sampler of Swivel weave on a two-block, four-harness Summer and Winter draft. Brown warp and tabby, pattern in black and white. Where pattern blocks alternate in color, there are weft floats on the reverse.

Page 101. Detail of photo on page 89.

Page 105. Detail of photo on page 35.

Page 111. Room divider in brown and white linen. Swivel weave on five harnesses, using floats as pattern, reversible. Detail on page vii.

Thrum, n. 1 (a) 1: A fringe of warp threads left on the loom after the cloth has been removed ...(2) one of these warp threads ...(b) loom waste consisting of warp ends and test fabric pieces ... 3: obsolete: a ragged beggarly lout

Webster's Third International Dictionary of the English Language, Unabridged.

ACKNOWLEDGEMENTS

Handweavers should have a Declaration of Interdependence because we are constantly learning from each other. If I were to list all the people who have helped me along the way it would take pages and include members of study groups, guilds who organize meetings and the speakers they have produced, the writers of our many books on the subject of weaving, participants in spontaneous midnight pow-wows, and many others who never heard of me. I have never met a weaver who did not produce some information that I needed to know, from the beginner who just put on her first warp to the internationally known expert.

Specifically, I would like to thank Virginia Brooks for reading the four chapters on dyeing, and Terry West for helping me to rewrite the last chapter.

I would also like to thank Leslie Burgess, who did the drawings, not only for her expertise as an illustrator, but for her encouragement and enthusiasm for the whole project.

DEDICATION

This book is for Woody, for his tolerance, support and (sometimes bewildered) encouragement that made it all possible.

TABLE OF CONTENTS

Introduction

"I make no claim to be an oracle: I am merely trying to pass along my findings and experience in the hope of being of some assistance to other craftsmen."
- Mary Meigs Atwater, **Design and the Handweaver.**

Being a handweaver over the past forty years has been an exhilarating experience. Even to one who knows herself to be just a hobbyist, it has been exciting to watch the field being developed from the first tentative copies of colonial weaves to the present time when weaving is again acknowledged to be worthy of classification as art.

This book is an outgrowth of a column written for ten years for the newsletter of the Potomac Craftsmen, and reflects my interest in the problems of beginning and intermediate weavers. You might call me the Heloise of the loom.

I have wrestled with the use of direct address, being an admirer of the deft way the British use the word "one" as a substitute for both "I" and "you." After reading Fowler on the subject, and not understanding most of it, I began substituting "one" for "you" in various phrases, finally arriving at the ridiculous "One can't take it with one," which is grammatically correct, but unbearably stuffy. So I have fallen back on the second person.

I have also wrestled with that bugbear of the English language, the use of pronouns in the third person singular. If any possible male readers of this book take offense of the consistent use of "she", consider how awkward it would have been to write "he/she" throughout. There are many talented, even famous, men weavers, but even-handedness has to stop somewhere short of prolixity. Let the men contemplate the fact that "he" is universally taken to mean both sexes.

The reader may find too much emphasis on ways of avoiding mistakes. In the words of W. S. Gilbert in *The Pirates of Penzance*.

We observe too great a stress
On the risks that on us press
And of reference a lack
To our chance of coming back.

The real truth is that I am not the most accurate of weavers. In fact, the late Stanley Zielinsky called me the most inaccurate person he ever tried to teach the drawing down of block weaves. Surely none of you will make all the mistakes I have, but if the book helps you to avoid even a few, I will feel it has been worth writing.

And your chances of coming back are very good, if you stay in touch with other weavers.

Handweaving As Mania

Handweavers tend to be clannish. If you are a fellow weaver, they rejoice in your company, and if you are not, they don't much care who you are.

If you are like many of us, you took up the craft mostly because you thought it would be fun to create something specific – bedspreads, rugs, curtains, place mats, scarves or clothing.

After learning to warp, treadle and throw the shuttle, the average addict goes through several stages.

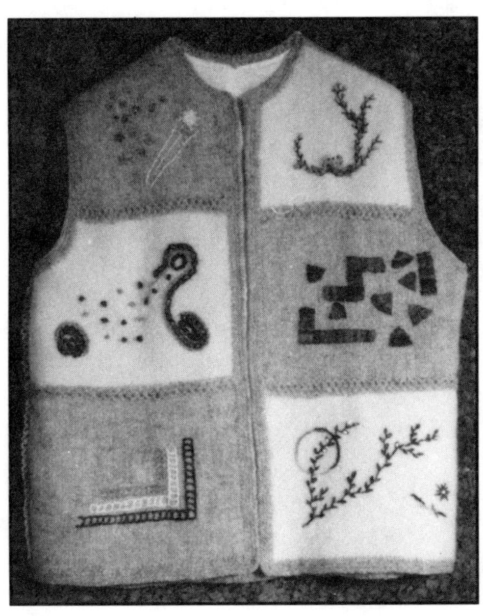

Stage One: You find out there is about a fifty-percent fallout among beginning weaving students because it's all a bit more complicated and demanding than they realized. If you are among the survivors, you acquire your first loom and discover that you have very little idea where to start on your own – what to weave, using what draft and what yarns.

Early on you are apt to be scared by the process of warping, so your first warp is much too long and the project may be abandoned, or finished at a disillusioning cost in boredom.

You are now fascinated by the whole idea of cloth and compulsively examine every woven thing you see – checking out the jacket in front of you at a concert to see how many harnesses it took to weave it. And you start collecting swatches of machine-woven cloth from fabric stores for their color and design.

Stage Two: Now you lean hard on projects with specific instructions and patterns. Like knitting directions, some are really challenging to your skill.

You start collecting yarns, books, and pictures of things you'd like to weave. You become interested in the history of weaving, which you are convinced is the history of civilization.

Stage Three: By now you've joined a guild for contact with others who share your mania. If there isn't one, you start one. You start taking workshops, attending conferences and joining study groups, and lay the foundations for lifelong friendships. You are now well launched on your lifetime hobby, career or profession.

This is the stage when, bit in teeth, you wouldn't dream of following recipes, which you regard as too much like shooting fish in a barrel. As a result you get yourself in trouble trying experiments that don't work, and learn the hard way to throw out disasters and charge the wasted effort and money to the cost of learning.

Stage Four: You become fascinated by fields related to weaving: spinning, interaction of colors, stitchery, or by specialties such as dyeing and warp painting. Or you discover that you like to teach because the interchange with your students results in your getting back as many ideas as you give.

You give up thinking of yourself as "Housewife" or "Business Woman" and tend to note on passport applications that you are a "Handweaver."

At about this point, the non-weavers you see infrequently are apt to ask, "Are you still weaving?" You are fully mature if you can repress the impolite counter-question, "Are you still breathing?"

Because of your obsession, you are in touch with many other weavers, so you overestimate the number that actually exist and forget that to the rest of the world you are sort of a freak. You may even be asked to mend a hole in a gabardine suit.

Stage Five: You have grown so accustomed to counting as you work that you find yourself counting when it is completely unnecessary, such as the number of strokes it takes to sweep the front porch.

You feel faintly uneasy when talking to anyone who doesn't weave – what is there to talk about? – and adopt esoteric terms such as "slabstock" and "argatch." Your idea of a real ball is to stay up all night at conferences and talk about weaving. You try to manipulate your family to spend vacations in areas where there is handweaving to be seen.

When you look at real estate advertisements showing floor plans for houses and apartments, you study them carefully to see whether there is space for a few looms.

Stage Six: You are truly over the edge when you find yourself enjoying the drudgery of threading a loom because you now find it helps you to relax from the tensions of everyday life.

Stage Seven: Many of us never reach this stage. You find yourself becoming a professional in the field of teaching, production, or writing, or in selling yarns, books and other people's finished products.

Probably the benchmark in this last stage is the point at which you have to report your earnings to the IRS.

The purpose of this review is simply to point out that whatever your reasons for starting this absorbing craft, the results will probably be quite different from your original intentions, and you may never get around to weaving those bedspreads, curtains, or placemats.

You'll never be rich, but as a Quaker friend says, "Weavers live to be a hundred and are happy every day of their lives."

Getting Started

If you're at a loss for topics among a group of handweavers (an unlikely situation) a sure-fire opener is, "How did you happen to learn to weave?" You will get a freshet of biographical material – more than you can handle.

Now in my case, the first handloom I ever saw was in a dining room in a house where we met with a group of square dancers. The piece being woven was a bright, large-scale plaid for curtains. In the light of later experience, I can't help wondering whether the pieces matched when they were put together.

A few days later I remarked idly to a neighbor that when our daughter started school, I might take up handweaving if I could find a teacher. So one autumn day I returned from a trip, with my kindergarten-age child by the hand, and was greeted by my neighbor at the front door with, "Our weaving classes start tomorrow night."

Within a year I had taken weaving lessons and bought a loom and a horizontal warping mill. How was I to know that learning to weave at that time was trial-and-error on a lunatic scale? That was in 1947, and weaving consisted of tabby, twill, lace, Summer and Winter, and overshot, especially the latter. We learned to thread a loom in Lily cotton and weave colonial patterns in wool weft, each block woven on the diagonal and squared, which we proudly called "tromped as writ." With infinite pains we learned to draw down the pattern blocks to visualize the overall design. People who know me will be surprised to learn that at the end of two sets of lessons I could design a coverlet, border and all. I could, but I never did, and nowadays I find it exhausting to think about.

Our teacher was slightly put out when I finally got hold of a twill threading in carpet warp and played with it, including (horror! not colonial!) adding supplementary warps hung from the back. Since I didn't know any better, I didn't take out the original ends in the supplementary warp area and the result was, to say the least, lumpy. In those days there were relatively few yarns suitable for handweaving, and even fewer designed especially for the purpose. Nowadays we can make more ambitious mistakes.

Shortly afterwards we started building a house, and while it was underway I wove a piece of upholstery in Rose Path to cover the back and seat of a simple chair. When it came from the upholsterer, I was mortified to discover that the pattern on the back was different from the rest, and it took me a long time to realize it was not my error. The upholsterer had put the material on the back wrong-side-out.

What goes into a new house? Why, stair carpeting, of course, and if you know only colonial design you think in terms of rag rugs. Since I was still afraid of the process of warping, my effort consisted of putting twenty yards of white carpet warp on the loom and waiting for inspiration to supply the design. The first half-yard convinced me I hated rag rugs, and there I was, stuck with the remaining 19 1/2 yards. So nothing was woven for months, until one day I came home from a meeting of the Potomac Craftsmen and found the loom empty – my husband had taken the warp off and destroyed it. I never looked back.

New rule adopted then and there: never put anything on a loom until your design is thought through, and make the warp just long enough for that particular project. Samples are, of course, another story.

The Potomac Craftsmen, then as now the guild for the Washington metropolitan area, met on Saturdays in the auditorium of the Smithsonian's Natural History Museum on the Mall. Its members turned out really impressive stuff in fine linens and wools. Some of the members tended to be a bit secretive about their work – what drafts and what yarns they used, and how they arrived at the finished product. If you were a raw beginner, taking notes and picking brains was frowned upon. So lacking experience or counsel, I designed and wove a set of Bronson lace place mats. I reasoned that if you wanted something un-colonial in really open lace, you used a singles linen and a wide sett. You might call this Disaster No. 2 (of dozens) in my weaving career. The mats were raggedy, not lacy, and simply fell apart.

At that time the many magnificent books we now have were still unwritten. There was nothing printed in color. *Handweaver and Craftsmen* started publication in 1950 and was a boon, but there were no color pages. Lily Mills was circulating a leaflet called "Practical Weaving Suggestions." If there were other periodicals, I never saw them. Texts included two classics: Mary Meigs Atwater's *Shuttlecraft Book of American Handweaving* and Mary Black's *Key to Weaving*, and those were all we had.

Mrs. Atwater also circulated a monthly mimeographed bulletin for which Harriet Tidball was doing much of the writing and editing. I never heard of it until much later.

In 1955 we moved to Minneapolis. It is never easy in a new city to find other weavers, and it took me some time to locate the Minnesota Weaver's Guild. (They later changed their name to Weaver's Guild of Minnesota for listing in the phone book, but that was not until after they had a permanent address for a telephone.)

Minnesota weaving was, and still is, heavily influenced by Scandinavian design, and very good design it is. The Guild taught beginning weavers at the local YWCA and at the University there were classes for occupational therapists with no room for hobbyists. For intermediate weavers there was no formal instruction and they were dependent on the help of the Guild in scheduling speakers, workshops and study groups.

Having struggled as one of them, my interest has always been on the problems of intermediate weavers, so I talked the Guild into letting me give short courses to pass on what little I knew to others who knew even less. One course, ambitiously titled "Interaction of Color and Weave," was aimed in that direction. The husband of one student remarked that it was the only 10:00 A.M. class that met at 9:30. The reason for the enthusiasm was that we started having long arguments about how to raise the general level of knowledge in the area. At that time the Guild had about 80 members, of whom fewer than half were actually weaving; the rest tended to come to meetings to talk about and listen to discussions on the subject nearest their hearts.

Our discussions eventually resulted in the formation of a weaving school. This took a titanic effort - buying more looms, finding a place to put them, organizing a faculty, raising money, and enlisting students. The members of our study groups worked like demons to get things started. Since I had the biggest mouth, I was appointed the first education chairman, and spent a whole summer planning courses based on the university system, with grandiose labels like "Floor Loom I, for Beginners," and "Floor Loom III, Projects." We ran scared that first year and broke even financially, to our great surprise. More important, the Guild membership doubled, and doubled again the following year. The school is still in existence.

One day at the school (which was in the basement of an old-style apartment house) a stranger walked in and asked whether she could teach rigid heddle weaving. We had never heard of a rigid heddle, but were ready to try anything. It was a huge success as an introduction to four-harness looms. The great development of weaving on rigid heddles was yet to come.

In the Fifties, California was under the influence of Dorothy Liebes, who was producing fascinating simple twills in wonderful colors with much emphasis on mixed warps, metallics and novelty yarns. The Yarn Depot in San Francisco was offering weaving classes in the new approach, taught by Cay Garrett. Two weeks with her, and seeing good handweaving actually used all over the city changed my life. The first piece I wove after returning home brought the comment from my teenager, "Well, you have finally woven something worth looking at." After only ten years of struggle, I found this very encouraging.

They say that teaching is a socially approved way of showing off how much you know. Being a show-off, I have often found myself on an informal hotline with some odd inquiries on the other end of the phone. For example:

Question: I bought some cotton yarn at a garage sale. Can you tell me how to set it?
Answer: What size is it?

Q: Oh, I don't know. Sort of string size.
A: Why don't you weave some samples?

Q: But I don't have time.

— and —

Q: My boy friend and I bought 20 pounds of Persian wool in several colors at a bargain price, and we want to weave a rug. How do you weave a rug, and can the wool be dyed so it all matches?

A: You can't just weave a rug by instructions over the phone. You need Peter Collingwood's book on rugs, and for dyeing you need the book by Vinroot and Crowder.

Q: Hey, we can't afford them.

— and —

Q: My house is carpeted in a color I don't like and it is faded in spots. It may be wool. Can I dye it on the floor?

A: Certainly, provided it is really wool and you can boil the house.

— and —

Q: I found an old loom in my mother's attic. Could you help me to find someone to teach me to weave?

A: Of course. How big is it?

Q: Oh, it's big. Can I bring it to your house?

A: (Thoughtful pause) Maybe you'd better describe it.

Q: Well, it's in four pieces that go together with wing nuts, and it has all these little brass nails all around, about a half-inch apart...

— and —

Then there was the voice of a distressed friend on the phone. She had been to Penland for a couple of weeks and was gung-ho about eight-harness twills. She complained that when she started to weave, the fabric came out all stringy. Help! A house call diagnosed the trouble. She had overlooked the significance of the eight-harness tie-ups and was trying to treadle the twill 12, 23, 34, 45, 56, 67, 78, 81. It was definitely stringy.

At the outset of this chapter I warned you that if you ask a weaver how she happened to take up weaving you get more information than you really need or want to know.

Tools Of The Trade

Engineers speak often of cams,
Chemists use terms such as "grams"
They'd be more comprehensible
If they said something sensible
About treadles and heddles and lamms.

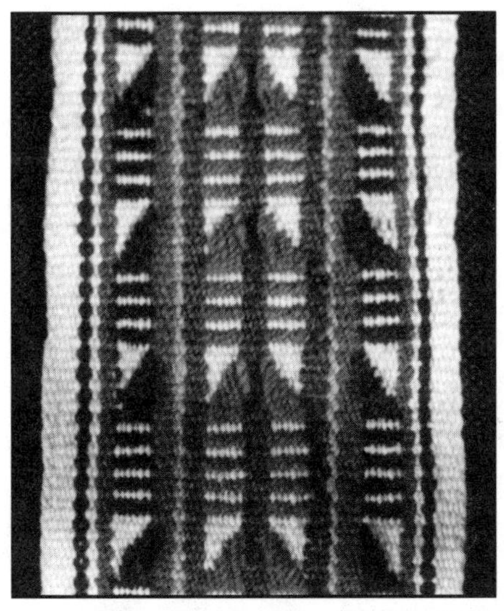

Buying your first loom is an awesome decision to make. One word of comfort, however: whatever loom you buy, you'll learn to love it, and if you outgrow it, you'll probably be able to pass it on to someone else. In this age of inflation, you stand to make a small profit. Looms are not like cars, which become "used cars" the minute you drive them off the lot. In fact, looms are more like horses; everyone has a favorite, and learning to manage it is part of the fun.

The smartest approach toward deciding what loom you want is to take weaving classes in which several types are used.

Ideally the loom for you should fit like a good pair of running shoes, but until the day when you acquire the perfect one for you, you can learn to weave on, and be inspired by, any device that makes different sheds.

Before you make up your mind, con as many of your weaving friends as possible into letting you try their looms. Manage to worm out of them what loom they would buy if they were acquiring another. Send out word that you're looking. A good hardwood loom almost never wears out (heavy use in weaving classes, though, can sometimes make even a sturdy loom rather shaky), and you may be able to find a second-hand one. Look in the classified section of your Guild newsletter, and even in the classified ads in your local newspaper. A family which inherits Great-Aunt Susan's loom may not have the foggiest idea of what it's worth or how to find out, and you may get a real bargain, sometimes with bench, books, small tools, and yarns thrown in.

A small loom is often a better investment than a big one. On the assumption that weaving is to be your lifetime occupation, you may want to own several, including a small one for samples and workshops.

Don't assume that "bigger is better." Bear in mind that if you are five-feet-two, your reach, including the length of your legs, is substantially shorter than that of a taller person. The harnesses have to be lifted constantly whether your loom has a weaving width of 20 or 56 inches. When Irene Wood wove the narrow samples for her book on multi-harness twills, her 20-harness samples were produced on a borrowed 56-inch Macomber. She had to remove the heel bar and weave by standing on the treadles (she weighs about 100 pounds soaking wet) because the harnesses were too heavy for her to lift from a sitting position.

Many a 60-inch, 16-harness loom is gathering dust because the harnesses are so heavy to lift that weaving is not fun, but very hard work.

If your space is limited you may be thinking about a table loom, but there are some disadvantages you should consider. Good (meaning heavy) table looms are nearly as expensive as small floor looms, and each requires a table which takes up its own space. A sufficiently sturdy table loom is cumbersome to move, since it must be lifted into place rather than pushed. Most important of all, it is hard to develop good weaving skills when all motions are with the hands rather than with both the hands and feet.

My own first loom was made in Oregon of Douglas fir, and had string heddles and a contramarch tie-up with sash cords which tended to stretch. A lot of my time was spent correcting loose ties, but the action of the loom was light and the sheds, when the tie-ups were correctly balanced, were a joy. However, once I graduated from overshot and twill to double weaves and multiple tie-up Summer and Winter, the difficulty of double tie-ups was a real obstacle. If you wished to weave unbalanced sheds with more than the standard six tie-ups you were in trouble, because the contramarch is so designed that you can't combine sheds by treadling with both feet. Regretfully I sold this nice loom to a friend who was sure she just wanted to weave twill on a standard tie-up.

The best thing about this loom was that it came with a very large and heavy warping mill, so I have never had to experience the toil of using a warping board.

The Minnesota Guild once inherited a Cranbrook loom - eight harnesses with cord tie-ups. Since, at that time, I was the only member who would admit to knowing how to tie up a contramarch, I was drafted for the job. (Contrary to rumor, that wasn't the real reason we left Minneapolis.) It was a day's hard work to make a complete tie-up, but the loom was a dream to work on. Nowadays, the whole process has been superseded by dobby attachments.

In the early Fifties there weren't all that many choices of looms. There were counterbalanced, with their problems in weaving unbalanced sheds. There were several jack looms, of which a favorite on the west Coast was (and still is) the Gilmore. That one I never could use because the treadles were wide and widely spaced. With my short reach, I couldn't depress a treadle on one side and throw a shuttle from the other. The Norwood, which is beautiful and still made, presented the same problem to a shorty.

My second loom was a revelation – a Macomber 40", and later, as a surprise birthday present, another Macomber, a 32" one, which has always been my favorite. One slight problem is that the Macombers have a short space between breast beam and reed, which is not great for weaving rugs but good discipline for anyone who tends to weave as much warp as possible before moving the fell toward the cloth beam. (Bad, bad!) The loom itself is plenty sturdy enough for rugs, however. I still have these two best-beloveds, and when my life gets too complicated for weaving I tend to walk by them and give them little pats such as you give a nice dog, and assure them I'll be back.

My Macombers came with the standard six treadles for four harnesses. When I added harnesses, I took Harriet Tidball's advice and got the maximum number of treadles the frames would hold.

The 32" has ten harnesses with room for two more, but let's face it: I seldom use more than four, or at most six, and much of my weaving could be done on two. With the extra treadles, I try to tie up the loom for a straight-across treadling order. In extreme situations this means eight to ten treadles with tie-ups repeated for straight treadling left to right. If you are ordering a new loom, you are most earnestly advised to request all the treadles the loom will hold.

If I were ninety years younger, I would certainly invest in one of the dobby or electronically controlled looms, and a computer with all that fancy viewing in color of a proposed weave: distant view, close-up, reverse of the weave, and who-knows-what.

When they invent a device that threads the reeds and heddles, I'll be first in line. I have often wondered who threads the looms in mills. Imagine setting one up to weave thousands of yards of 200-count percale in a width to go on a king- sized bed! Apparently mills depend on tying on to an existing warp, but still that's a mind-boggling number of knots.

There have been some pretty wild looms in the past, starting with the type pictured on Greek vases with Penelope standing before a vertical loom, with sword in hand, beating upward. The hanging warp was weighted with stones for tensioning. That type of loom was used in the more remote areas of Scandinavia until relatively recent times.

In Japan you see pictures of looms with the warp stretched on a frame pegged to the ground and the weaver kneeling before it. Then there are African looms where the weaver (usually male) works on a warp stretched on the ground away from him, with a big stone tensioning the warp. In Greece I saw weavers working at looms with the warps wound in oval-shaped form like a bobbin, instead of a perfect cylinder such as we require. I lie awake nights trying to figure out how they keep even tension.

In Japan, in a moment of euphoria, I ordered a fascinating Korean loom, which arrived as a bundle of sticks, so to speak. It was a giant three-dimensional puzzle until I found a museum publication with a good sketch of the loom in use. It was essentially a backstrap loom in that the tension was maintained by a curved piece of wood which went around your hips. You sat on a low shelf which was part of the loom. The shed was changed by pulling back one foot to which was attached a cord running to one shed. The Japanese weave in two standard rather narrow widths, for kimonos and for obi, and this is really a quite efficient way to weave.

If you've ever woven on a huge loom from colonial times, you have discovered that the heavy overslung beater is a joy: the weaver simply pushes the beater away and lets it come forward of its own weight. If the fell is moved forward frequently so that the reed strikes it at nearly the same angle every shot, an even beat is a breeze. There are not many of these homemade looms around. Most of them are in museums or period restorations such as Williamsburg. The explanation for their disappearance is simple: when machine-woven textiles began to appear, the housewife joyfully adopted them at once. Weaving wasn't an art, it was a chore, and involved coercing the children to sit around the fire at night winding bobbins. So the space-consuming monsters were gladly abandoned and their parts stored in the attic or the barn. Came the day when a large cured timber was required on the farm, the old loom was there, cut and smoothed and ready for the taking; the string heddles and the reed would be of little value for recycling, so they disappeared.

There is a tradition among Virginia weavers that dogwood was a favorite wood for shuttles because it doesn't splinter when dropped. The story goes that when a son was born to a plantation family, a dogwood grove was planted. When his college tuition had to be met, the grove was harvested and the wood sold to the burgeoning mills along the fall line. Even if this legend isn't true, it deserves to be. Dogwood grows wild on Virginia mountainsides. In the spring, the woods are breathtaking with white flowers.

There have been some pretty weird looms on the market in modern times. In the summer of 1952, the *Saturday Evening Post* carried an article about a new one, and there are a few of them still around. It was made of shiny aluminum pipe, built to weave about 20" wide, and measured about 20" from breast to back beam, standing on short legs. It was well designed for its purpose – occupational therapy, with special reference to bedridden patients – since the legs were just long enough to allow the loom to fit over your lap. Sheds were changed by a wheel arrangement which was within easy reach. The warp was wound by the manufacturer, and when it ran out, the warp beam was packed up and shipped to the company for rewarping.

All well and good, but the author of the article in the *Post* got completely carried away. He claimed that (1) anyone can make a living by selling handwovens; (2) it was the only loom that would do "circular weave," by which he meant tubular double weave; and (3) it was an advance on the floor loom because it was very short from front to back, whereas floor looms are too long and therefore require lease sticks. To compound the felony, he advised his readers not to consult experienced handweavers because they are very secretive about their knowledge.

This nonsense quite certainly was not the fault of the manufacturer but, in revenge, insulted handweavers dubbed the loom "The Pipefitter's Dream." Dozens of people who had never heard of handweaving before fell for the line. A well- known school of art in the Midwest bought 20 or so of "The Pipefitter's Dream," at $250 each, a tremendous price at the time. They arrived warped, and when the warps were used up, the looms were stored and eventually given away.

If anyone ever telephones you to say, "I was given this nice loom and I'd like you to teach me to warp it," be very suspicious. Ask for a description; it might be the Pipefitter's Dream. It might be warped at home by someone with an inventive mind who could make and use a warping drum, so you might enjoy the adventure.

It could be really great if you like to weave in bed.

A perfectly respectable company, which shall be nameless, once designed a loom with a metal frame. At their request I tried it out, and since it was billed as "good for rugs," put a 20-inch linen warp on it. The tension necessary for rugs was too strong for it, and the metal beams (front and back) bent out of shape. (In fairness, it is probable that this would not have happened with a full-width warp.) It is hard to visualize the amount of strain a strong warp under tension can place on front and back beams. This loom had a very short life on the market.

Some time ago, the Handweaver's Guild of America (HGA) had some material printed for promotion, including a cute postcard with cartoon-style sketches of a weaver's work space – spinning wheel, swift, yarns in skeins, tubes and balls; plus four children, one dog and several cats. (Obviously the studio's owner was Superwoman.) Pride of place was given to a sketch of a threaded loom. The warp is correctly shown coming from the warp beam, over the back beam, through harnesses and beater to the breast beam, but from there it sort of reversed, never reaching the cloth beam. Even more interesting, the shed was shown open (without a fell) and the bottom half of the shed was level, while the raised warp created a shallow inverted V.

I once tried to weave on just such a loom in England, with the warp running level through the reed and heddles from front to back beam. When the shed was opened, the upper part tightened and the lower part loosened, so every time the shuttle was thrown, it caught up parts of the lower half of the shed, making weaving a perfect nightmare. On a jack loom, either the back beam should be higher than the front beam, or the harnesses should be heavy so that their weight holds the warp down, and the lower half of the shed holds tight against the shuttle race.

Some years back the Smithsonian Institution had a nice, life-size diorama of a prehistoric village, including a woman weaving a band using a slot-and-eye rigid heddle. It was very well done, with the tension on the warp produced by attaching it to the foot of the weaver, who was seated on the ground. The only trouble was that the rigid heddle was down by the woman's ankles, well beyond her arm's reach. I wrote a cranky letter to the museum but never got a reply and I haven't been in the building lately to check. They probably get a God's-plenty of letters from Know-It-Alls.

I quote from *Connections* by James Burke and the television show of the same name: "On this new loom, the threads were stretched horizontally on a frame. The horizontal boards above the frame each supported two more horizontal boards with holes in them. Through the holes in one board passed the even-numbered threads of the warp, while the odd-numbered threads passed through the holes in the other. These boards were lifted alternately by the use of foot pedals attached to the overhead supporting boards.... The speed of weaving on this loom was much greater than the old vertical one, and production rose fast."

If Mr. Burke's description had included the observation that one of the boards had slots, he might have been describing a sort of rigid heddle loom, but it's a safe bet that he failed to visualize the topological situation when trying to get a board to pass through half of the warp. He can be forgiven, however, because he later gives credit to the Jacquard loom, via the Census Bureau, for the ideas that gave birth to the computer.

Now that these complaints are out of our system, let's go back to your new loom. Once you have it, you must start to collect the equipment you need to start weaving; bench, shuttles, warping devices, reeds, skeiners and swifts (not the same thing), scissors, books, plus a whole host of odds and ends that you can improvise at practically no expense. In fact, it is possible to become a collector of small weaving tools that you never use but love to own – peculiar shuttles, oddball reeds, antiques.

Benches: The height of your weaving bench is the most important thing about it, and that's a personal matter, depending on your height and reach and, to a great extent, on the dimensions of your loom. Before you buy a bench, try different seats and stools until you can decide which is best for you. The Macombers require a high bench, at least for me, and I found the perfect answer at the Midwest Conference – an adjustable height and a sliding seat over an open box so I can store filled quills on one side and empty ones on the other, along with things I use frequently, while occasionally used items are in the center. The seat had to be padded so I wouldn't slide off it into the storage space. A friend of mine, who weaves weft face rugs and hangings on a 60-inch loom, has a very slick wide bench and slides across it. An old-fashioned piano stool which winds up and down to change height would be a real find. If you can borrow one, it would help you to decide which height is most comfortable for you.

Reeds: If you buy a second-hand loom, it will probably come with several reeds, but a new loom usually has only one, in your choice of number of dents per inch. The #12 is probably the best choice, but if you are buying several, you might want to consider some of the reeds that have an odd number of dents per inch, for instance a #7 or #9. It is easy to sley 4, 6, or 8 ends to the inch in a #12, but the odd-numbered dent reeds give you more leeway in varying sleys.

Harriet Tidball's *Weaver's Book,* has a chart of the possibilities of varying ends-per-inch using various reeds. You can easily make such a chart for yourself, listing vertically the number of dents per inch of various reeds, and across the top the possible sleys: 1-0, 1-1, 1-2, 2-2, 2-3, and 3-3. Generally speaking, how much you vary the sley depends on the weave and the yarn, because a sley such as 14 epi in a #12 reed can sometimes, but not always, create reed marks which do not finish out. Reed marks are mostly a problem in closely set plain weaves using tightly spun yarns.

Back in the Fifties, most looms came with a #15 reed, since weavers at the time concentrated on fairly fine cottons, linens, and wools set at 30 epi. A veteran weaver in the early days of the Potomac Craftsmen once complained that she was being plagued by moths and couldn't find the source. All was made clear when she acquired a coarser reed; in installing it she found years of wool lint and moth eggs, in the grooves of the beater. She had never moved the 15-dent reed since her first warp.

For double weaves, coarser reeds are better than fine reeds, and the present fad for huge or lumpy yarns definitely calls for coarse reeds. If you are a rug weaver, an extra-heavy #5 or #6 reed is a boon, but there's a catch – stiff linen yarns have a deplorable habit of slithering out of the reed after it's sleyed.

Shuttles: This would probably be the next concern of the new loom owner. They come in many curious shapes and sizes for specialized purposes.

The standard is the shuttle with the rotating bobbin. Even they come in many shapes as the result of different requirements: pointed, blunt, heavy, light, tiny, huge, and/or single- and double-bobbins. For this type you really need a bobbin winder, either hand or electrically turned, unless of course you plan to put your children to work and put them through a training course so they can produce a bobbin that won't cause you grief when you throw the shuttle. There are shuttles with rollers on the bottom, but the throw is not really improved over the slick-bottom type.

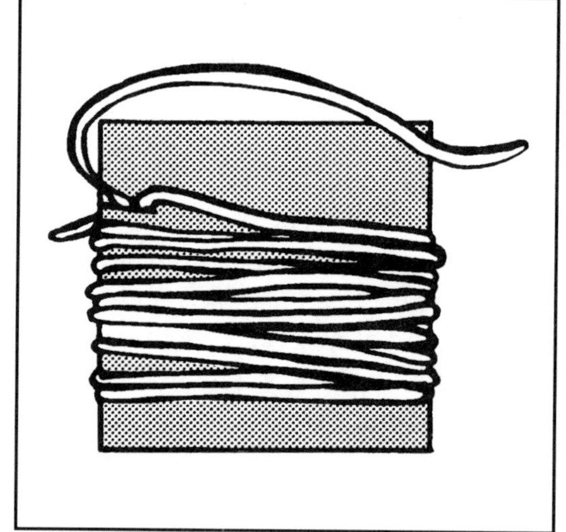

If you are weaving bands or narrow samples, standard wood shuttles have an irritating habit of falling to the floor. A better carrier of the weft is a 3-inch square of good cardboard with a slit on one corner to hold the start of the yarn. These little shuttles are also useful for inlays or many changes of color in the weft. Tapestry weavers can use them, too, because a corner of the square serves well in bubbling, and they stand upright in the warp. The cardboard should be approximately of the quality of poster board, but can be recycled from boxes and packages. (I like Red Rose Tea packages, myself.) They can also be handy for permanent storage of small amounts of yarn.

If you weave rugs, you will probably need ski shuttles unless you can find improbably large bobbin shuttles. Maybe you're a real pioneer type and can use stick shuttles. These should be longer than your warp width, since they can't be thrown.

I am sorry to report that some of us are addicted to the end-feed shuttle which is expensive. Filling the pirn is most easily done by using a special bobbin winder which has support for the pirn at both ends. This is the shuttle used in mills, but the handweaver's version is much lighter.

The end-feed shuttle has two great advantages – it holds a great deal of yarn and, unlike the rotating bobbin, the yarn doesn't pull in the selvage as the throw is getting up to speed, hence better selvages. While you're getting your feet under you in weaving, get regular boat shuttles and put the end-feed shuttle and its bobbin winder on your wish list. Not everybody likes them, as they take a little getting used to and the tapered pirn is wound quite differently from the standard rotating bobbin.

Warping Devices: Warps can be wound on most anything – legs of upside-down chairs to horizontal warping mills. In the middle is the standard wall-hung warping frame which can be made at home, but I would like to put in a word about the horizontal mill. With mine, I can make a 25-inch, five-yard warp in several colors in two hours or less, without fatigue; in a single yarn, less than an hour. It is made of Douglas fir and ordinary hardware, and is unnecessarily large for my purposes because, as a beginning weaver, I was thinking in terms of weaving curtains, mad fool that I was. It can be dismantled for storage, but I generally keep it folded against the wall, where it takes up very little space, and it assembles so quickly that I use it even for very short warps. The main requirement for a good horizontal mill is that it should not tip over as it is spun (anchor it to floor or table) and it must be at a height which does not tire you. Mine has been copied several times by handy husbands.

Swifts and Skeiners: An umbrella swift is a traditional implement for the weaver. The Victoria and Albert Museum in London has one worth stealing, beautifully decorated with painted flowers on enamel, and obviously someone's cherished heirloom. Ordinary undecorated ones are not so lovely but very useful. Have you ever focused on the rigging, though? Recently some of the little string ties on mine all wore out at once, and I had to figure out which stick should be tied to which.

Swifts have only one purpose – to hold a skein while it is unwound. They have the great advantage of holding skeins under a gentle, even tension even as the diameter enlarges as the skeins grow thinner.

On one of our family excursions to see some of the old restored plantation houses in Virginia, we were shown a kitchen which also housed a loom, spinning wheel, and weaving tools. (Lots of lint in the stew, no doubt.) There was a niddy noddy which is perfect for skeining, but the guide stated that the swift was used for measuring yarn. After we left, our daughter complimented me on my unusual restraint in not correcting the speaker: a swift is a clumsy instrument for winding skeins and useless for measuring them. It simply takes the place of an extra pair of hands while you wind a warp, ball, or bobbin from a skein.

A good strong skeiner is useful both as a swift and a skeiner, but it should be adjustable for different circumferences. If you are a dyer you really need the adjustment possibility if you use it as a swift, since skeins shrink in dyeing.

Ball Winders: Which brings us, by natural sequence, to the indispensable ball winder. It is inexpensive, but most of them have plastic gears which make them quite short lived. If you wind balls by hand it takes forever. With the ball winder it is easy to make a center-pull ball from wool. Tightly twisted, fine or slippery yarns, though, tend to tangle when pulled from the center. Toilet paper cores placed over the shaft will produce a core to hold such yarns. You can write any necessary information above the yarn. If the core is too small to fit over the shaft, simply slit it partway up.

Lights: You need a good light over your loom even if the overall light is good. The best kind is the architect's lamp which is supplied with a clamp and jointed in several places so that it can be adjusted to put light where you want it.

Set-up for Supplementary Warps: At a study group meeting recently, one of the members was describing her problems with a sample warp, and said she was embarrassed at the mess at the back of the loom where she took some ends out and added others, hanging them from the back beam and weighting them. Well, now. Embarrassing? On the contrary, creative. Harriet Tidball once described a visit to the mills at Galashiels, Scotland, where many of the textiles used in Paris are woven. She said the design looms looked like a weaver's nightmare, with strings and weights all over the place. If it's good enough for Galashiels, it's good enough for us amateurs.

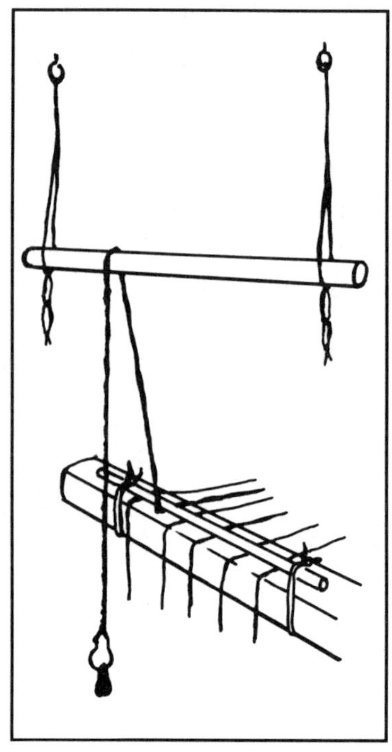

Extra warp ends can be threaded through reed and heddles, hung from the back beam and weighted near the floor. During weaving, when the weights rise to the back beam, they can be moved down to the floor again. While weaving a long piece with supplementary warps, I grew tired of all this running around, and invented what Leslie Burgess, who drew the line drawings for this book, calls my "trapeze." It consists of two dowels and some long cords. One dowel is suspended from the ceiling just within reach, and one is tied to the back beam on top of the foundation warp. The supplementary warp runs from front to back through reed and heddles, under the back-beam dowel, up over the ceiling dowel, and down to the floor. It's a longer time between adjustments, and it is easy, while seated, to see the weights as they rise.

My present work space, through no fault of my own, has a 12-foot ceiling, so a dowel suspended from it is out of the question. One winter day, when my built-in handyman was suffering from a golf deficiency, I devised a demountable trapeze which I thought would entertain him sawing wood and boring holes. The result was disappointing as a time-user; it took him just two hours including a trip to a lumber dealer. The principle is simple, consisting of two 1" x 3" boards tied to the uprights of the back beam to support the upper dowel at a height suitable to a short weaver.

One unanticipated benefit of the design is that since the upper dowel slides into holes in the uprights (held in place by cotter pins) the device can be attached to any width of loom and is easily disassembled and stored in a corner. The sketch may help you to visualize this.

Some looms have two warp beams for weaving two sets of warps with different tensions, such as tucks and seersucker. I have a loom with this feature, but have found it exasperating to make the rather subtle adjustments between the two tensions.

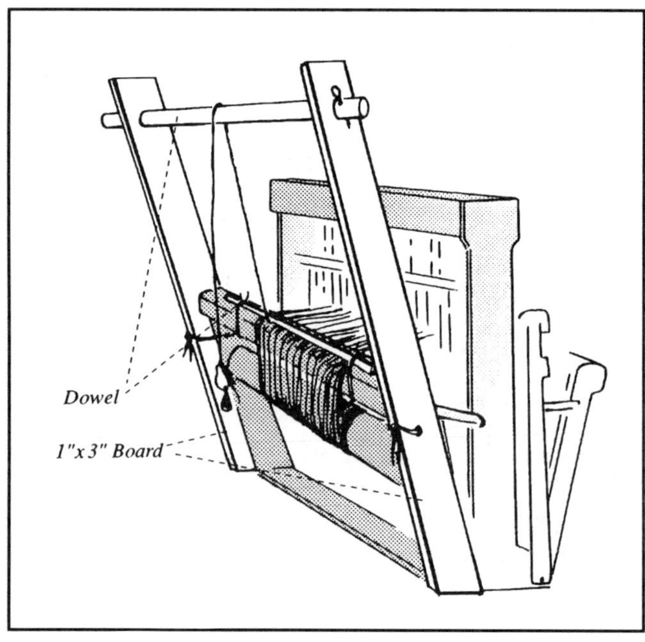

Adding supplementary warps is a bit tricky. Since I work from the front, I sley and thread both base and extra warps. While the basic warp is being rolled onto the warp beam and tensioned, the supplementary warps are tied over the castle out of the way. After the base is finished, the supplementary warps are pulled through to the back, passed under the warp-beam dowel, up over the upper dowel and down to the floor. They are then tied in at the cloth beam, and the ends combed and tensioned. You could add them after the base warp is threaded and tensioned, but you must leave empty heddles in the right places during the process to carry the supplementary ends. Remember that the supplementary warp must be longer than the base.

This method wouldn't be very practical for tuck weave or seersucker, but several times I have used the set-up for a series of garments with changes of color in the stripes.

Keyhole-shaped, metal shower-curtain rings plus fish weights or big washers make good weights for tensioning groups of yarns. They are threaded onto the larger part of the ring, and the narrow end goes through a slip knot on the end near the floor. The ring closes like a safety pin, and rises as the warp is moved forward. For groups of threads you need a surprising amount of weight.

Scissors: These have an invisible means of locomotion and when you need to cut a single end, you find they have burrowed under the flotsam and jetsam. So buy yourself some single-edge razor blades and scavenge some fairly thick cardboard. Cut a piece of the latter the width of a blade and twice the height, score and fold the cardboard, and cut a very small notch in the center of the fold. Insert the blade so the sharp edge is in the fold, and tape the other three sides of the rectangle. The cardboard will protect you from cuts, and the tiny piece of exposed blade will cut any yarn of reasonable size. Attach a piece of string to this little gizmo and install it near your bobbin winder, skeiner or whatever. You can distribute these cheapies wherever you need them and postpone hunting for your scissors.

A pair of scissors on a length of bias tape can go around your neck to save some of those *now where did I leave my scissors this time* moments. Bandage scissors have one open end for the fingers and can be hooked over a pocket or your neckline. One blade is longer than the other and is blunted, which avoids the tragedy of accidentally putting sharp points in the web and also guards against stabbing yourself when you sit down. And besides, the scissors are so distinctive in appearance that they are easily spotted when misplaced (as in stolen) by some unprincipled member of the family for some unauthorized (as in nefarious) use.

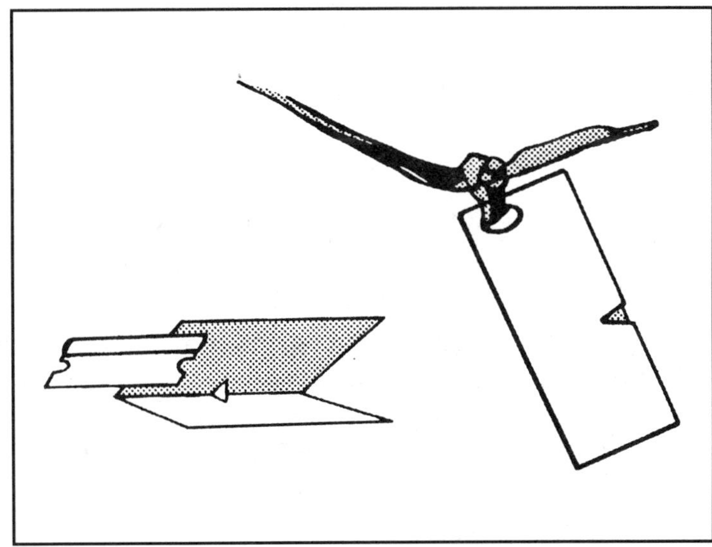

Clippers, rather than scissors, are handy to have near you while you weave. There are expensive types, but the best are very sharp, black clippers made in Japan, which are much less expensive and cut better. If you have a quilting friend, inquire about sources.

Measuring and Measuring Devices: Weavers spend much of their time measuring. Here are some simple tricks to make your life easier:

Bore a hole in a yardstick and hang it on a wall where it's handy, and remember to put it back.

Get some cheap tape measures and glue them in various places: the front of the beater below the shuttle race, the back of the beater, and the edge of your work table.

The exact center of the beater can be marked with a thin slice of colored sticky tape, both on the shuttle race and in back of the reed.

Mark the center of each reed with a bright thread.

A sewing gauge from a fabric store is a big help. If you can find one made of steel, it will stick to a small strip magnet glued to the castle; if it is aluminum, a small hook will hold it.

Heddles: A friend of mine, Janet Stollnitz, had a brilliant idea for handling the very lumpy yarns, which are often sprinkled across the warp for emphasis, but which are sometimes too big to go through a regular heddle eye. She bought some tiny plastic rings at the variety store and tied them as heddles on the harness frames so that the rings serve as heddle eyes.

Correction Heddles: (Let's hope you will never need them.) Those of steel can be bought, but it is easier to tie a temporary string heddle to fit your harnesses. If you need several of them, make a heddle block and keep it for future reference.

Note that the string is long enough on the loop end to enable you to put it on the steel support in a snitch knot. The two knots forming the eye are usually grannies, and the heddle is tied on the top steel with a square knot.

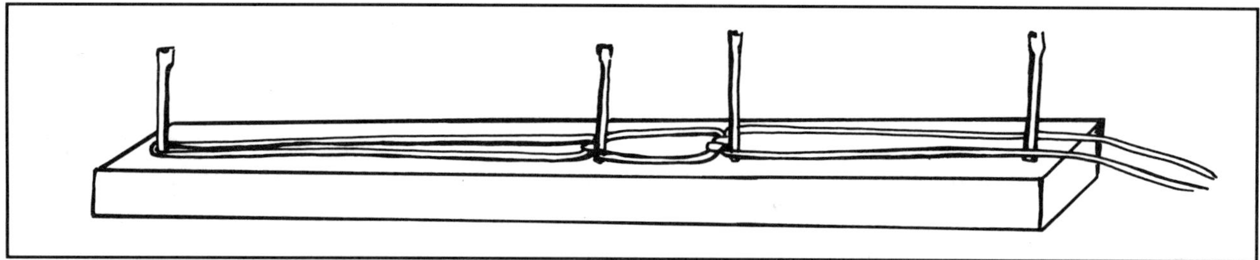

Reed Hooks: A reed hook is a tool that you must have at hand for various chores such as correcting errors after the warp is on the loom but years ago, inspired by a monograph on weaving tweeds, I taught myself to thread heddles by a method which is more accurate (for me).

First, divide the draft into manageable groups (a unit of pattern or an inch of width in the reed). Then, mark each group with the number of ends and heddles needed for that group. As you thread, count out both threads and heddles in each section.

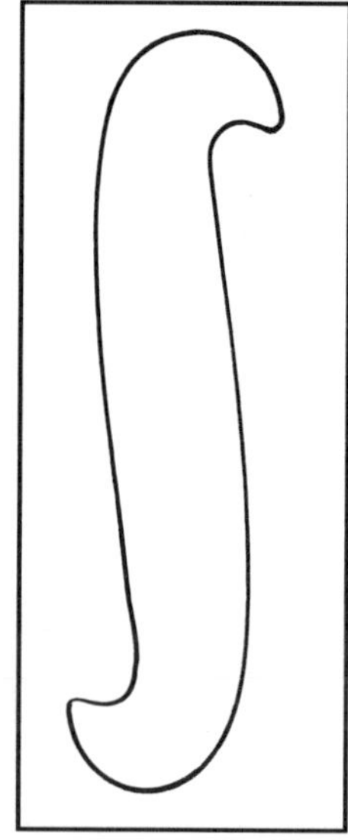

A group of warp ends is held in tension with three fingers of my right hand, reserving thumb and forefinger to steady the heddle being threaded. With my left hand I select an end, pull it up into a loop, and selecting a heddle with my right hand, put the loop through the heddle eye. (The left hand has to be coerced into learning to do this.) If heddles and ends in the group don't come out even you have made a mistake, but it is necessary to backcheck only that group. It is clear that I will never win any speed contests but very seldom is it necessary to rethread any great number of ends.

For sleying the reed, I use an S-shaped, hand-whittled hook of wood which came with my first loom. It is so thin, it will not distort even a fine reed, and in case of fire, it is first on the list for rescue. There are metal versions of this, but they have a tendency to fall out of the reed because of their weight, so plastic versions are more practical.

The late, great Stanley Zielinsky, in the process of threading a loom, was a sight to behold. He stood astride the breast beam and, with an extra-long reed hook, threaded reed and heddle at the same time with one masterful stroke.

Spool Racks: When under the delusion that I was going for long fine warps, I acquired a sectional beam, and a spool rack which has only been used once for its original purpose. Now it is one of the most useful things in my workplace. A swift is mounted on the top, and on one side is an adjustable steel skeiner. The rack stores spools of various strings and ikat tape, plus a device called Grip-A-Strip which holds sheets of paper with such information as color schedules and warp layouts for reference while at the loom. The rack is very stable and can be moved about easily.

Fastened to the spool rack, below and to the left of the skeiner, there is a C- clamp. When a skein is being wound from a cone, ball or tube, the yarn is placed on the floor just below and to the left of the clamp. The yarn is held just above it, and then goes down under the grooves of the clamp, from where it is accurately fed upward onto the skeiner. Two clothespins on the grooves of the clamp keep the yarn in a narrow channel.

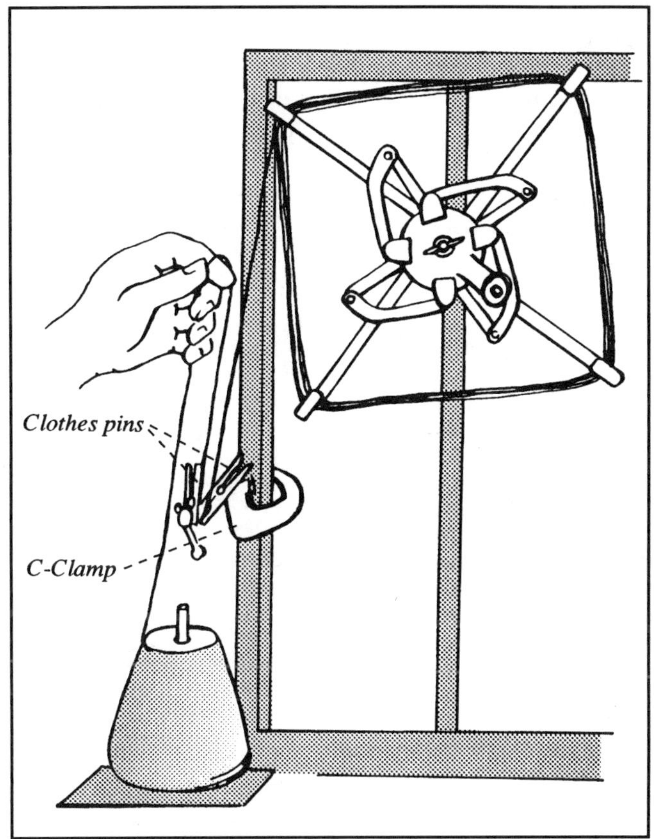

Warp Padding: Sticks and paper are usually used for padding the warp to keep it cylindrical so all the ends are the same length. Heavy paper lasts a long time, but sometimes it can roll on with creases that create small but cumulative differences in the diameter of the roll. Some chain warpers advocate using a long roll of corrugated cardboard the width of the warp beam. I never seem to be able to start it perfectly straight, so have always used sheets of plastic the width of the beam and 18" long. (A cut-up shower curtain is less slippery than the shiny type.) But this, too, is hard to start without wrinkles at the beginning. After years of struggle, an idea surfaced: the leading edge of the plastic is stapled to a stick. If the stick is straight on the beam, the plastic follows it neatly.

The operative words here are in the statement, "If the stick is straight on the beam," for failure to place the sticks exactly level can create a fractional difference of the roll at one end. This problem was solved by driving two long screws into a 2" x 2" board, which is taped exactly level on the warp beam. The sticks at the head of the plastic sheets extend out beyond them. If they rest firmly against the screws they are straight. Of course the completed warp is not now the prescribed perfect cylinder, but more egg-shaped in cross-section.

In case you think all this is an unnecessary amount of fuss, consider: if a stick is not absolutely level it can cause a slight difference in diameter in the rolled warp. If this is, say, one-fourth inch, every time the warp is unrolled one turn, the length will be one-fourth inch longer on one side than the other. In ten turns, your warp will be 2 1/2" longer on one side than on the other – a real headache.

SLICK TRICKS

- Spring clothespins are very useful to have on hand to use for everything from grouping warp ends to weighting threads.
- A bulldog clip fastened to the castle right in front of your eyes makes a good device to hold notes for frequent reference. And bless the man who invented "Post-It" notes.
- A niddy-noddy is ideal for making short sample warps. Usually you don't need a cross, but can simply cut the skein and pull the ends out of the bundle one at a time for threading. Most niddy-noddies make a two-yard warp, but if you cut the warp in two, you have double the number of ends, one yard long. On many looms, this will weave about 15 inches of samples.
- For a whole series of samples in different colors, you can tie one short warp to another just finished. Tie in front of the reed, roll the new warp back and tie in at the front.
- The most convenient place to store sticks and paper or plastic is on the loom itself. Roll it all into a compact bundle which can be suspended from a lower cross brace at the back of the loom.
- A sectional beam can be converted temporarily into a smooth beam by placing a firm roll of corrugated paper over the pegs.
- King Charles's Head* for sectional warpers is how to count the turns on the beam so that some sections don't turn up shorter or longer than the rest. One solution is to measure one warp end for each section the exact length needed, spool and place it on the rack. When the measured spool runs out, the section is complete.
- A collection of shoelaces, all lengths, hung where you can reach them, can be used in all sorts of ways for quick ties. They are designed to be tied and untied easily and have stiffened ends which go through small openings such as reeds and heddle eyes. Get odd-colored ones or dye white laces freakish colors to prevent their being liberated by spouse or children for emergency use on shoes.
- Plastic-covered wires, such as come with fresh vegetables from the market, make good emergency ties. Long pipe cleaners from a hobby shop are even better and easier on the fingers.
- A corset string, if you can find one, is endlessly useful.
- A gallon plastic jug can be standard equipment for winding warps or bobbins. Cut a large hole where the handle is, but leave the hole at the top intact. Put a ball, tube or cone in the side opening, bring the yarn through the top hole, and your yarn won't roll all over the floor.
- If your reeds are not stainless steel, clean and spray them with silicone and they are as good as stainless steel, and a lot less expensive. This treatment also works for the steel heddle bars that hold the heddles, which will eventually rust in a damp climate.
- Beware of using masking tapes, and some transparent tapes, on your loom. If left on wood for very long, they will ruin the finish. Scotch Magic Tape is harmless to finishes, and if left on for a long time can be removed with cleaning wax. (This writer is *not* subsidized by the 3M Company.)

* "King Charles's Head" is a phrase applied to an obsession. It comes from Mr. Dick in Dicken's "*David Copperfield*", who, whatever the subject, always came back to "King Charles's Head." I had to look it up, too. The Editor

- Kitchen cleaning wax is useful to have at hand if your tools have a varnished surface. Coffee stains instantly disappear with its use.
- Empty tissue boxes, particularly the tall square kind, are ideal depositories for the pesky clipped yarn ends and skein ties that are such a nuisance to discard.
- I have an ugly, but useful, three-legged plant stand made of wood and reed which is placed beside the loom for materials to be used for the work in progress: warp, weft, clipboard, pens, and what have you.
- A handy thing to keep in your loom bench is a stenographer's notebook for rough notes to be torn out and used as raw material for records on a project.
- If you feel persecuted because you have only a narrow loom, here are some suggestions for projects:

  Bands – warp face, overshot, pick-up patterns

  Towels

  Place Mats

  Scarves

  Shawls - can be made wide by joining narrow strips

  Double width weaves

  Clothing made of strips or squares or diamonds joined together

  Bags and purses

  Rugs, woven in strips and firmly joined.

Yarns, Your Raw Materials

Support your local yarn dealers; you need them, they need you.

To the true fiber fanatic, yarn is anything that has two ends and bends a little. Besides the classics - wool and hair, cotton, silk, linen, rayon and synthetics - there have been yarns made from some unlikely substances.

Spider silk and milkweed have been spun, but proved unsuccessful. Forty years ago there was some yarn on the market which was made from milk - don't ask me how. Wire has been, and still is, used in weaving. Asbestos has been tried, and let us be thankful that it never really caught on. Spun glass had its day, but a weaver who did extensive research on it wound up in the hospital with a dangerous rash. Plastics in the form of monofilament are widely used for special purposes, and mylar combined with aluminum produces a yarn which glitters but does not tarnish. Gold and silver were used far back in the past in textiles of incredible luxury for royalty and the very rich, but very little cloth of gold has survived, since it was all too easy to melt it down for the metal. If you've ever seen an ancient work of art woven with silver, it most likely was a sad and dull object. West Coast Indians used a mixture of cedar bark and wool.

Yarn lovers have a deplorable tendency to accumulate and hoard the object of their affection, and many of us who have been weaving for years have a stockpile that would require a lifetime to use up. To quote Anita Mayer quoting somebody else, "The weaver who has the most yarn when she dies, wins."

Sooner or later we all buy yarns on impulse, only to find out that they don't seem to fit into any project we can devise. Here are some typical solutions to such problems:

Wrong color: Any of the natural fibers, plus rayon and nylon, can be overdyed. A too-bright color can be toned into a more acceptable hue by dyeing it in a very light solution of gray or brown. Pastels can be dyed to darker or brighter colors with results not too different from the same dyes on natural whites. A yarn spun of natural fibers with synthetics, or combinations of cellulose fibers (cotton, linen or rayon) with wool can be dyed to produce tweedy or heathery effects – acid dyes will color the wool and leave the cellulose fiber white or very pale, while fiber reactive dyes will color the cellulose and leave the wool white or light. The results are often a pleasant heathery effect.

And for the most fun of all, try skeining a lot of fibers, disregarding both color and type, and dyeing them all in the same bath. You'll be surprised.

Too fine: Textiles with a very soft hand can be produced by winding several fine ends together for warp or weft, and combining fine yarns in several colors can have fascinating results. Blending colors in this way is a trick well known to tapestry weavers.

Fine yarns can also be included with heavier ones to modify the texture or color. If the value contrast is not too great, fine yarns can shift the over-all color slightly without being noticeable in the finished article.

Different dye lots: Sometimes yarns can be obtained at a really low price because they are a mixture of dye lots – this is particularly true of sales on knitting yarns. Even natural colors in yarn come in dye lots – beware! Knitters would probably be well-advised to avoid such bargains, but weavers can use several dye lots in one warp by sleying the different lots at random (warping from the front, of course) while being careful that several ends of the same dye lot are not sleyed side by side to create a strong stripe.

The solution is not so easy in the weft. Sometimes it is possible to disguise the change of color or value by rotating two or more shuttles at the point of transition from one dye lot to another.

If you just don't like the yarn: Swap. One weaver's dog is another's treasure.

Too little for a project: Don't overlook the value of small quantities of leftover yarns, or even dye samples. A few ends of a different color or texture can bring a design to life.

And don't forget your colleagues, the embroiderers and tapestry weavers, who covet yarns in quantities too small to be obtainable from yarn dealers. A gift of thrums, useless to you, can win friends and influence people.

Yarn Counts

Most of us are resigned to the confusion in size, yardage and loft of various fibers, and are forced to struggle along with experience and experiments to decide which yarns at which setts will make satisfactory textiles.

Take for example cotton and linen. Size 20/2 mercerized cotton makes a fairly fine textile set at 30-32 ends per inch, while 10/2, 8/2 and 5/2 make rather heavy materials. In fact, 5/2 mercerized cotton makes excellent place mats set at l8 epi. You might conclude that comparative counts in linen would produce similar results, but you would be wrong. 20/2 Linen makes a heavy fabric suitable for place mats. For a sheer linen for clothing or curtains, you need 40/2 or finer.

In wool, a 20/2 worsted, sett at about 30 ends per inch, makes a light fabric. This starting point is not very helpful, since there are several systems of counting the yardage of wool. In the States we use a different size system from that of Europe, and in England there seem to be at least two different counts, presumably because machine spinning of wool started up in different areas and those counts became set in concrete.

The knitter can produce samples in a very short time to determine the proper density of a fabric, but the process is much more laborious on the loom. If you buy knitting yarns and depend on designations like "knitting worsted" or "fingering yarn," you can be in real trouble. The only safe guide to wool is the number of yards to the pound or skein, plus experience in the fulling process.

You can also get into trouble if you calculate yardage of yarns for a specific project and rely too much on the stated number of yards per pound. Bear in mind that the yardage given by the manufacturer is based on the measurement of one pound of that yarn in a single ply. Plying shortens the measurement of length quite substantially. So do yourself a favor – be generous in your estimates.

Storage

Once you start buying yarn, whether for specific projects or on irresistible impulse, the problem of storage rears its ugly head.

Weavers of rugs and tapestry like to keep their yarns on open shelves where their colors form an inspirational background, but this is not for those who dislike adding more dust to yarns that were probably dusty when they came from the mill. Some of us store yarn by color, some by fiber, and some by size. No matter what your system, sooner or later it will fail you: Now where did I put that blue worsted or have I used it all up? The answer may require the dismantling of your entire storage area.

Clear plastic bags are one solution, although experts at the Smithsonian Institution caution you about storing precious fabrics in sealed plastic which causes them to deteriorate. Plastic bags on open shelves, even though the colors can be dimly seen, are not all that inspirational, especially when dust accumulates on the bags.

I herewith make you a present of my system - not the best but the one I can manage. All yarns are in plastic bags to keep colors and dye lots together. They are then placed in standard transfer files, which are sturdy boxes measuring 12 by 15 by 10 inches, with lids. As a concession to esthetics, the boxes are covered with Contact paper in an imitation of wood. Each box is numbered and labeled and I try to keep an up-to-date inventory of the contents.

The inventory took several days of toil to get started, and is not too well kept up, but it's better than nothing. Yarns are classified as follows:

Wools: singles; fine-plied; medium-plied; heavy-plied; small quantities of left-over yarns, and dye samples

Silks: heavy-shiny; heavy-dull; fine; noils; colored; dyeable

Cottons and linens: colored; natural and white (dyeable)

Rayons: all sizes and colors

Unspun yarns: Lopi; sliver; silk caps

Samples of these yarns are snitched through holes in the side of cardboard sheets which are punched to fit a three-hole binder. Alongside each yarn is a notation on size, yardage, source, price if I remember it, plus remarks as to its uses, sett, reaction to dyes, and so on.

I am not a slave to this system, but it takes a lot less time to keep it fairly organized than the days when I had to turn out every cupboard to find what I was looking for. Sometimes I forgot completely what was squirreled away.

A confession at this point: I may not remember your face or name, but hand me a six-inch sample of one of my stored yarns and I can tell you how long ago I acquired it, the approximate price, and add information such as "I bought five pounds of this silk from Contessa in 1969; it cost $16 a pound and dyes well."

About Moths: This household had a near disaster when a much-used Mexican rug was stored in my yarn cupboard. I called an exterminator and was told that there is no such thing as general fumigation for moths - the professional has to find the source and deal with it. So I destroyed the moth-eaten rug, dumped all my yarns out on a sunny lawn and reorganized their storage. If you find a tube or skein with ends sticking out, indicating the presence of moths, get rid of it and start checking all your wools, alpacas and mohairs. There seems to be some argument about the value of cedar storage for warding off moths. If it really works, the cheapest form consists of cedar shavings from a pet shop.

If you feel guilty about the space taken up by your yarns, you should know about a former neighbor who kept a box labeled "String not worth saving." Feel better?

On the theory that one good plagiarism deserves another, the following was stolen from the "Design Quarterly" of the Minnesota Weavers Guild:

Creative Yarn Storage

(Note: this column was plagiarized by the Fiber Source Committee members from Kay Sorense in Paddock Lake, Wisconsin, who originally wrote it for fabric collectors.)

How to hide your yarn from your husband, who can't understand why you need all that yarn:

Here are ways you probably use already:

- 1. In the attic
- 2. Under the bed
- 3. In closets, drawers and boxes labeled "baby clothes" and "Christmas ornaments"

Here are some additional ideas for really desperate yarn junkies:

- 4. In garbage cans (new, of course)
- 5. In the trunk of the car, until you can sneak it in the house while he's sleeping on the couch
- 6. Black plastic garbage bags - be careful though, if anyone in your house is helpful enough to carry out garbage
- 7. In luggage (really good if you never travel). Just be sure your husband does not take the wrong piece of luggage on his next business trip
- 8. Hung on a hanger in the closet with a dress or blouse over it
- 9. In the freezer or an old empty refrigerator (especially good against moths), or if your freezer is half empty. A full freezer is more economical to run.*
- 10. In boxes labeled summer china and winter china
- 11. Out on an open shelf in the family room, or weaving room if you're lucky, arranged like a rainbow. Now it's a collection, not your obsession.

***Comment from the author:** This statement is a typical self-deceptive justification found in the true yarn addict.

Wool and Hair

Wool, beloved of hand spinners, weavers and knitters, probably has more variations in type and texture than any other fiber. In the form of yarn it ranges from fine filaments combed to lie smooth and parallel, to fuzzies and huge plies, or singles bigger than your thumb. Hair comes from a surprising variety of animals - Angora rabbits to long-haired cattle, not to mention your pet Samoyed.

Wool and hair can be soft or extremely harsh to the touch, as in hair shirt. Sometimes yarn manufacturers treat it to be machine washable.

Nobody really knows how long wool and its variations have been spun, but the process surely goes back to prehistoric times.

In 1976 at Convergence, one of the speakers, from the cool region of Denmark, expressed surprise that very few of the conferees were wearing handwoven clothing. The answer was quite simple: many of us like to work in wool, and since Convergence is always held in hot weather we tend to leave our woolly masterpieces at home.

Question: why is wool the odds-on favorite with handweavers, spinners and knitters? For one thing, wool is very sympathetic to handle, and it dyes readily with home methods, adapting to stunts such as variegated color. Because wool is clingy, its setts can easily be varied from open to very close, and even in open setts it can be squared in the weaving.

In recent years the types of spins have been burgeoning and range from thin-smooth to lumpy, bumpy and fuzzy. Their spins keep their characteristics through long use.

We are spoiled by the ease of care of some synthetics, but wool clothing also packs for travel with a minimum of permanent creases, coming closest to synthetics in this regard. Wools blended with synthetics are especially easy to care for.

Unlike cotton, which absorbs soil, wool microscopically sheds it. In some weaves wool wears so well it is just short of immortal - a quality which is less highly thought of in our throw-away culture than it was in the time of our ancestors when garments might be worn for two generations and then wind up as very long-wearing rag rugs.

Harriet Tidball's *The Weaver's Book* has pages on setts for the various natural fibers, but none for wool, the reason being that wool is so adaptable that it can be woven in a bewildering number of setts. If you want such a table for wool, you'll have to produce your own, according to your personal experience and preferences.

Wool is widely imitated by various synthetics, particularly in machine knits. There are crucial differences, though. Most wool will not pill, and many of the imitations do. Synthetics do not full well and many are not pleasant to handle.

The majority of fibers classed as wool come from sheep, and have been important articles of trade back into prehistory. The classic Roman toga was woven of white wool.

This brings us to a topic dear to the heart of the handweaver – the domestic sheep.

It's possible to grow up in the midst of an industry and learn nothing about it, either because it doesn't seem interesting or because your parents and teachers assume you must know all about it. I grew up in sheep country and though several of my classmates came from big ranches, I never thought to inform myself about sheep. Most of what I know has been learned as a weaver.

For one thing, the term "shepherd", as used in the Bible, is never used on a sheep ranch. The man in charge is a sheepherder. In my day in the West, he was usually a Basque (I have no idea why) who spoke little English and spent weeks on the high summer range alone except for his sheep and his dog. Sometimes, at state fairs and horse shows, you can see demonstrations of the amazing abilities of sheep dogs. They keep the flock together partly by instinct and partly by following instructions given by signals such as whistles.

Birds come in flocks, cattle come in herds. In the West, sheep come in bands. So why are those in charge called sheepherders? It's a mystery.

Many sheep ranchers wouldn't be caught dead eating lamb and mutton, and I doubt if it's out of love of their beasts.

Lambing is an anxious time, since sheep don't plan very well; lambs are born when the weather is unkind to them. Mother sheep and offspring sometimes don't recognize each other, so each ewe and lamb are put in a little pen until they acknowledge each other. Sometimes this measure fails, and the orphans are called "bum lambs." If the rancher's wife and the ranch cook are kindly persons, their warm kitchens are apt to house several babies, baa-ing away for their bottles.

Sheep are considered to be extremely stupid, but it's hardly their fault. They have been hand-tended for thousands of years and bred not for brains but for wool and meat. Hence they have become unable to fend for themselves. In fact, a sheep with a full coat of wool, especially if wet, cannot right itself if turned upside down, and, without help, will die that way.

To illustrate how little I knew about sheep B.W. ("Before Weaving"), some years ago we were at a restaurant with a group of Montana friends, and since the steaks were huge, we asked for doggie bags. As the waitress passed the bags around, she asked each of us how many dogs we had. The man at my right, whom I had known for years, said he had 22 dogs. Amazed, I asked why, and he said "Twenty-two bands of sheep, 22 dogs."

Again amazed, I asked how many sheep in a band? His answer was "Two thousand." Whereupon my caustic brother-in-law leaned across the table and said, "The next thing you ask him is how much money he has in the bank."

Of course, in Australia a mere 44,000 sheep represents a small outfit.

Further trivia about sheep, if you're still with me:

Newborn lambs in the field are hilarious. They bounce in the air as if they're on springs.

In the West, the term "sheep-killing dog" expresses hatred. The term is sometimes applied to obnoxious persons.

"Sheepdip" has a technical meaning – tick control and disinfectant – but can also refer to bad whiskey.

Some owners of sheep who raise them for fleeces to sell to handweavers, such as the River Farm on the Shenandoah, put plastic ponchos on their sheep to keep them clean and dry. (One wonders whether the sheep appreciate this thoughtfulness.) The mind boggles at the thought of putting raincoats on 44,000 sheep.

A surprising number of people, even weavers, don't seem to know the difference between worsted and woolen. Both are wool, but worsted is made of the longest fibers, combed so that they lie parallel and can be spun into very fine yarn; most men's suits are woven of worsted. Years ago I bought an English raincoat of worsted; it is lightweight, sheds water very well, and might be taken for silk. Woolens, on the other hand, are carded so that the fibers lie every which way, producing a soft bouncy yarn which can be easily dyed, and woven into lightweight but thick and warm textiles.

Under the classification of hair there is an extensive class of animal fibers including mohair, cashmere, cowhair, alpaca and its princely cousin vicuna, which are classified as camel hair.

Some of these yarns, such as mohair, are produced from the guard hairs of the animal. Mohair is very difficult to full, so it is often combined with wool yarn. Fulling must be done with a certain amount of caution and – guess what? – sampling. Most mohair is used in fuzzies, but it is possible to find it in flat-spun, very strong yarn. It is extremely slippery, however, and hence hard to use as warp. Knots just untie themselves.

Clouded Crystal Ball Department: back twenty-five years ago Harriet Tidball, fresh from a visit to Galashiels, warned a group of weavers not to put their money into mohair, as it was about to go out of style.

The dictionary defines cashmere as the inner hair of the Angora goat. Most of what we see in the States comes from the Himalayas, and oddly enough, from Kashmir.

Alpaca is a soft and silky fiber from one of three New World camels - llamas (which produce poor material for spinning) alpaca and vicuna. The latter have never been domesticated so (they say) the rare yarn is the product of fibers picked from bushes. The alpaca is quite commonly seen in Andean countries. They are tame and quite attractive, but it's advisable not to approach them too closely. I encountered one in Machu Picchu that was busily engaged in keeping down the grasses on one of the terraces. He looked so handsome in his future yarn hanging down in loopy, not too clean, strands, that I walked up and cooed at him. He spat in my eye.

Then there is the musk ox from above the Arctic Circle. It provides a rare yarn called qiviut spun from the undercoat, a fiber more soft and luxurious than cashmere. A few years ago the Smithsonian Magazine had an essay on this attractive beast, with pictures. Only one bit of information was provided about qiviut fiber, stating that it is softer than cashmere and the entire production is used by Eskimo women who "weave" (meaning knit) caps and scarves from it. Very few of us in the "Lower 48" have had a chance to touch this marvelous fiber. Some years ago at a conference I happened on a group sitting on the grass around a young woman who had a collection of knitted scarves and a handful of the unspun fiber. She had been a guest on a farm in Arctic Canada where the owners were raising musk oxen and supplying the local Eskimo knitters with yarn. The herd was quite tame, she said, but tended to be skittish at the approach of a stranger. One day when she was in the field near the herd, she heard a loud sound, like a shot or a car backfire. She was thrilled when the musk ox herd surrounded her, standing in a protective circle, horns outward.

The American bison is a large and dangerous animal which stands six feet tall at the shoulder. It provides no fiber for spinning, and is approached on foot only by the foolhardy. The musk ox is much smaller and is described in the Smithsonian article as a cuddly beast, something like a very large gerbil. They thrive on the treeless tundra of the Arctic where there is little snow. Their coats are so warm that they suffer from heat stress at anything above 50 degrees, so if you're thinking of raising one in your back yard, forget it. Nor is there much likelihood of finding qiviut at your friendly neighborhood yarn dealer.

Scandinavian weavers often use a yarn that is called "cowhair" which is really cowhair mixed and spun with wool, very useful for rugs because it wears like iron. It is hard to visualize a cow that would produce a fiber long enough to be spun. I didn't quite believe in it until I saw some Highland cattle in Scotland, covered with long droopy coats.

Spinning is a craft which has made enormous progress in the immediate past. Some years ago at a Midwest conference I was approached by a weaver from St. Louis who asked whether the Minnesota Guild accepted spinners for membership. Astonished, I asked, "Why not?" She said firmly, "Well, we don't," and marched off quite offended.

Can you stand more spinning stories?

A renowned Canadian spinner once appeared at the Michigan League conference driving a van with a license reading "Ewe Haul."

At a Folk Life Festival, an annual event in Washington, D.C., a spinner who was watching a mountain-woman spinner asked her how she washed her fleece. After some thought the spinner said, "I prefer the Maytag."

And a local spinner was demonstrating her art at a craft fair, displaying some fibers useful for handspinning including some dog hair. She explained that the Samoyed undercoat made particularly soft and light yarn. Two women in the crowd looked at her disapprovingly, and as they walked away one remarked to the other, "Too bad she had to kill her dog."

Cotton

When I learned to weave, cottons were the least expensive yarns for handweavers, and there was some propaganda to the effect that wool, linen and silk took more skill than beginners could handle, so they started with cotton. It is true that cotton is very sympathetic to the hand. At that time it came in many forms (mostly smooth) and in many colors.

These days cotton is not inexpensive, and we antiques look back with sadness to the days when the perle or mercerized cottons came in 125 glorious colors in five weights: 20/2, 10/2, 5/2, 3/2, and floss, and cost about $5.00 a pound. Specialized spins came in a smaller range of colors. In general, cottons were a weaver's mainstay.

It is true that wool suitable for clothing comes in many spins, dyes beautifully at home, and results in a textile that packs and wears with minimal creasing. However, a good mercerized cotton garment will be cool to wear and will also pack nearly crease-free. Fortunately the fashion world is helping us by popularizing knitted cottons, which means that there are some leftovers for handweavers and knitters.

Cotton is, and probably always has been, the most-used fiber in the world. It was developed from wild plants in the new and the old worlds.

During our Civil War, when England was cut off from American cotton, mill workers in Lancashire, England had a very thin time indeed, so dependent were they on American cotton.

The middle American areas in pre-Columbian times were completely dependent on cotton for clothing. If you look at the Mayan stelae carved with figures wearing very elaborately decorated clothing, you are seeing a rendering in sculpture of cotton garments. Archaeologists don't seem to agree whether the surface decoration is embroidery or weaver-controlled brocade ("pick-up" to you), but my money would be on the latter.

Quilted cotton cloth was worn as armor by the warriors of Mexico. It wasn't terribly effective against the firearms of the Conquistadors.

There were no sheep in the New World until they were introduced by the Spanish. The Andean civilizations, of course, had alpaca, but apparently there were no animals in semitropical Central America which produced a coat long enough to spin.

A recent popular book on archaeology speculated on the decline and fall of the great city of Teotihuacan near Mexico City. The author surmised that the city was abandoned because the surrounding country became too arid to support it. He then proceeded to paint a sad picture of drying fields and dying sheep. Teotihuacan was a ruin by about 800 A.D., seven hundred years before sheep were introduced,

As workers in fiber, we might look back on Pre-Columbian America as a paradise for spinners and weavers - their products were so treasured that textiles were used as currency and the really expert worker was a valued citizen.

The next time you use a sewing machine, think of the miracle of machine-spun cotton. A spool may contain 125 yards or more, so evenly plied that if the thread breaks because of an uneven spin, you feel entitled to be furious. Think of the incredible skill of the engineers who devised the machinery that can spin with such consistency, and the quality control that must be exercised.

While we're admiring modern technology, let's have a sad thought about inflation. Some of my spools of sewing cotton are museum pieces from a former life when I thought sewing was fun, and prices were so steady that they were imprinted right on the spool, like 15¢. Later spools of the same size are marked with paper labels, say 30¢. Then inflation took over so that the labels do not mention price.

Linen

Linen also has a long history, its origin lost in time. Today it can be classed as a very expensive yarn. Flax, the raw material of linen, grows nearly everywhere but its processing into yarn is time and labor consuming and it is expensive to dye. It is still much admired, as witness the synthetics that imitate it in appearance, if not in performance.

There are a couple of problems with handwoven linen besides its expense. It makes nice clothing if you don't mind looking wrinkled or pressing your garments every time you wear them. My personal addiction to synthetic blends (which save much time for weaving) is not cured by the word from fashion gurus that it is stylish to wear wrinkled linen, showing that you know what's what and never mind the expense.

Time was when linen place mats were a staple of classy gift shops. Nowadays a shopper who will pay $150 for a dress to be thrown away after a few months' wear won't spring for a set of place mats and napkins, at the same price, which would last in daily use for a couple of lifetimes.

Setts are very important in linen. Set too close, the textile will be very hard to launder. In any case it looks like gunny-sack on the loom and its real beauty doesn't appear until after severe washing and hard ironing. But don't, the first time you wash it, spin it in the washer for more than a minute or so, or you will set creases which cannot be laundered out.

Linen is preferred for dish towels because they do not deposit lint, but not all linen has this quality. Wet-spun linen is nearly lintless, but tow linen is about the lintiest fiber extant. Some years back, a company in Oregon developed a heavy tow linen which was widely touted as "thirsty linen." Some handweavers produced bath towels of this yarn, amid much sneezing from flying lint, and found that their washers became clogged with lint. Big disaster.

Currently there is a lot of fashion propaganda for clothing made of ramie, as if it were a new invention, but it has been on the market for years and is merely a linen made, believe it or not, from a species of nettle.

Rayon

We tend to think of rayon as a synthetic fiber, but it actually is classed among the cellulose yarns with cotton and linen. It was initially used to imitate silk, but it can be spun to look like wool or linen. As a yarn for handweavers it is relatively inexpensive and it takes fiber reactive dyes the most readily of all fibers. However, it has serious drawbacks: it is weak when wet, textiles made of it crease badly, and it is very heavy. If you compare the yardage of a silk yarn and that of a rayon closely imitating it, you will find that rayon is not the bargain you thought.

Fashion designers are currently using much rayon in designs that once called for linen, wool or silk. Recently I bought a black skirt – well designed and not cheap – under the impression that it was fine wool. It turned out to be a real headache because it must be constantly pressed and packs so poorly that it is useless for travel. It is made of rayon spun to closely imitate fine worsted wool. On the other hand, rayon spun with synthetics can be very practical, especially in the form that resembles heavy linen.

Silk

Since ancient times, silk has been considered the ultimate in fibers, as witness the phrases that have become part of the language – "silky hair" and "satiny skin." It has always been, and still is, the most expensive of the fibers used in spinning. Until recently there have been no really successful imitations of silk, and even now polyesters cannot match it in some important characteristics.

This writer grew up in the state capital of Montana, formerly on the main line of two transcontinental railroads. The town is built on the side of a mountain, and trains passing through the valley below could be seen and heard for miles. As far back as I can remember, when a fast train rushed through without stopping people said "There goes the silk train." Before the late Thirties, when nylon was invented, all women who could possibly afford it wore costly silk stockings, which wore out very quickly, so the consumption of silk was enormous. Silk coming from the Orient was sent by ship to Seattle and loaded on special trains which were given the right of way clear across the continent to the eastern mills. Even passenger trains were sidetracked to let them pass, because the insurance cost was so high the owners couldn't afford to have the silk on the way any longer than necessary.

When Japan attacked Pearl Harbor, there was a fully loaded silk train en route from Seattle, but suddenly war materials took over the highest priority. My father was then an official of the state government and was asked by the shipper in Seattle to find storage space for the train's cargo. The local armory was rented for the duration and the silk stored there. It was said to be quite a sight, with every level stacked from floor to ceiling with bales of silk.

By the time the war was over, nylon had taken over the market for stockings, since they can be snagged or cut but practically never wear out. I've often wondered what became of that trainload of silk and regretted that I didn't have enough information to inquire in what form it was, those fabulous bales.

You may have seen a Christmas film called "Amahl and the Night Visitors," which was an opera written for television. It was about an extremely poor widow and child who were visited by the Three Wise Men who were clad in sumptuous clothing, while Amahl and his mother wore very realistic rags. The Walker Art Center organized a show of these costumes and it was a shock to discover that the "rags" were made of sheer silk which drifted about in interesting tatters.

We may as well give up correcting clothing salespeople who point out that certain garments made of slubby silk are "raw silk." Don't confuse them with the facts: raw silk is beige in color and contains seracin, a natural waxy substance which stiffens the yarn so that in the skein it might be mistaken for some form of synthetic.

Handweavers have to admit that we are at the end of the yarn production line. That is, when there are leftovers from the factories, some kind spinning company thinks of us as a possible market for quantities too small for the big mills. Because of the dearth of silk for us, there was until recently relatively little information available to weavers and knitters about the handling of this wonderful fiber. Cheryl Kolander's *Silk Worker's Notebook* remedies this situation and is heartily recommended to those about to try working with silk. She does not, however, go into the subject of dyeing.

Silk has always been regarded as a cool-to-wear fiber. This is only partially true. The long filaments of silk can be spun into extremely fine-but-strong yarn used to weave sheer textiles which are cool to wear. In itself, silk is nearly as warm as wool. The winter kimonos of Japan used to be, and perhaps still are, padded with unspun silk, said to be as warm as down and less bulky.

There are many variations of silk yarn - some are tightly spun and plied, and some are lofty and fluffy like wool. There is a also lot of difference in the wearing quality of silk yarns. Be aware that some of the shiny, smooth, bulky yarns used as satiny accents may turn dull if subjected to abrasion; this is because the filaments are not really long, but carefully combed to produce luster, and abrasion may raise tiny ends which make the textile look dull.

There is more silk noil on the market than lustrous silk, and it is much less expensive. The reason is simple: noil is spun from what you might call spinning leftovers - short fibers produced along the way as the longer filaments are combed for spinning. Noil is rather weak, and singles are apt to break if used as warp, so it should be tightly spun and preferably plied to weave well.Noil has all the beautiful drape and hand of the more expensive silks without the luster.

A smooth, plied, lustrous silk might be regarded as ideal material for very simple and elegant garments. It ain't necessarily so. A plain-weave cardigan (you know – let the material speak for itself) in heavy, undyed, spun silk was the dullest thing I ever produced. Do knitters really appreciate their advantage in being able to salvage the yarn after such a disaster? Still and all, silk is magic to weave and, if it weren't so expensive would be the right stuff for beginning weavers.

When you look at a cone or skein of silk, it may look too fine to handle. Since it tends to expand when relaxed, however, silk with an apparent grist of a cotton sewing thread doesn't necessarily have to be set at 60 ends to the inch. You're tired of being told "Weave a sample," but since there are really no standard setts for silk, and spins vary so greatly, weaving and fulling a sample is almost the only way to avoid wasting very expensive yarn.

Once I undertook to weave enough heavy silk to make a white dinner jacket for my husband, using a plain, smooth silk and a slub silk, both size 5/2. The original idea was to warp a half-inch of slub alternately with a half-inch of smooth, and weave it to form checks. Some instinct of caution led me to weave and full a good-sized sample, and make the discovery that the areas of slub-crossing-slub puffed up more than the plain-crossing-plain so the sample came out looking like some peculiar form of seersucker. Because I had the wit to weave a sample, the warp was wound in the plain and the weft thrown in the slub. It made a sensational jacket.

When you are looking at silk and shrinking from its cost, you might also look at its yardage and sett. The 5/2 silk at 1200 yards to the pound sets very nicely at 16 epi for a firm but flexible twill. A 10/2 cotton has the same yardage per pound but the standard sett is 27 epi in twill, so the difference in cost, while considerable, is not really out of sight. The jacket warp weighed about 16 ounces off the loom. I won't harrow your feelings by revealing what it cost back then. I hate to see weavers cry.

The sad outcome of this adventure was that while the jacket was greatly admired, the wearer complained that when the weather was warm enough to warrant wearing white, the textile was too warm to wear. Those are times that try a weaver's soul.

Although silk is so magical to weave, it does have certain drawbacks. When wet, some silk has an unpleasant odor. The yarn has a mysterious habit of forming knots all by itself, and is so full of electricity that when a warp is wound, the part between back beam and heddles can arch up in the most alarming way. When chaining or winding bobbins, you can hold a sheet of fabric softener in your fingers to reduce static. (If you think we have trouble with static electricity in the winter in the East, try living in Minnesota, where on a cold day you can walk across a wool carpet to turn on a light and get a long stinging spark from the switch. Friendly dogs lead a hard life.)

Very delicate silks can be sized. Recipe (stolen from Cheryl Kolander): 2 tablespoons of mucilage glue, 1 cup of water, 1/8 tsp. of vinegar. This can be diluted and used to soak skeins; it washes out when the textile is woven. Ms. Kolander says it is harmless to silk and she has other recommendations for sizing in the woven piece. She also suggests that the darker naturals in silk can he bleached to cream white with Peroxide. My experiments have been very successful. Peroxide tests as mildly acid, which seems to be harmless to silk.

Sometimes a silk fabric is so limp and slippery that it is very difficult to cut and sew. An idea that works is to press it before cutting with a light spray of "Magic Sizing" from the supermarket.

The natural colors of silk range from a dark beige to pure white, depending on the species of the silk moth and what they eat. Some of the colors are not at all beautiful. For years I have been hoarding three big cones of the ugliest, dullest, grungiest, lusterless beige you can imagine. Using hydrogen peroxide in the amount of two liquid ounces for each ounce of yarn, covering the yarn with water, and simmering for an hour, produced a lovely, pale, creamy beige. The big surprise was that the bleached yarn was almost shiny and quite lofty, which means it can be used in an open sett.

Synthetics and Blends

On the market these days are yarns in mixtures of animal fibers, vegetable fibers, rayons, and synthetics. Sometimes these mixtures partake of the best characteristics of each component. For example wool-and-nylon bouclé is very stable and easy to dye, and makes a light but warm and thick textile for clothing. Mixtures of linen and rayon make a good heavy fabric, but both fibers share the tendency to result in textiles that crease and require a lot of maintenance.

Pure synthetics that imitate cotton, silk or wool somehow don't quite make it. Imitations of silk are hot to wear because they are nonabsorbent, and sometimes are unpleasantly shiny. Imitations of cotton and wool have a nearly universal tendency to pill, and in fact there are little electric shavers on the market to remove the pills. Most are impossible to dye by home methods; nylon is the exception to this because it dyes with the same chemicals that dye wool. As yarn for handweaving, synthetics stretch and recover like wool, but do not full into acceptable fabrics. Nylon alone has almost never been made into a yarn that can be knitted or handwoven successfully.

Very likely the makers of synthetics would like to put cotton, flax and sheep out of business, but so far the best they have come up with is a multitude of new types of yarns created from a combination of naturals and synthetics. The makers of knitting yarns have been especially busy, and a visit to your yarn shop may put you into a tizzy trying to choose from among the overwhelming

Weaves And Warp Finishes

A time-honored gambit for essayists (perhaps desperate for a topic) has been to ask the question, "If you were marooned on a desert island, what one book would you want to have?" A variation on this for handweavers would be, "If you could have only one four-harness draft, but an infinite choice of reeds, setts, yarns, and colors, which draft would you choose?"

The answer for many of us is easy: the straight draw twill, that is harnesses threaded 1, 2, 3, 4 and repeat, which is the first draft usually given to beginning weavers. Let's see what variations are possible on this set-up. Starting with balanced plain weave: log cabin with many intriguing variations; basket; an infinity of variations in color and texture including stripes and plaids; tiny patterns in color. Carol Kurtz in her book, *Designing for Weaving* and Helene Bress in *The Weaving Book*, have shown us a dizzying number of patterns produced on plain weave by manipulation of colors in warp and weft.

To this list you can add the hand manipulated weaves, often called "lace," such as Brooks Bouquet, gauze, leno, Spanish Medallion, and Spanish Eyelet. Harriet Tidball's *Two-Harness Textiles, the Open-Work Weaves* is probably the most comprehensive text on these.

Plain weave with an open sett: on this set-up the weft is beaten down to cover the warp, and it is the foundation for rugs and tapestries. There are so many possibilities that they occupy at least 167 pages of Peter Collingwood's *Techniques of Rug Weaving*. Many of the techniques are applicable to textiles other than rugs: meet-and-separate, inlay, soumak, and chained wefts are only a start.

All this before we get to twill treadlings - here the possibilities are enormous. In rugs, Collingwood has many small repeat patterns formed by changing the color and order of the wefts: 13 pages of these, with pictures.

If you are using a smooth yarn for warp and weft, you can weave a form of lace on twill by treadling 13, 12, 13, 12, 13 for one block and 24, 34, 24, 34, 24 for the other. If you shorten each block by two shots (e.g. to 13, 12, 13 and 24, 34, 24) and alternate the blocks, you get a nice wavy line and small openings, very useful for creating open areas. If beaten down solidly, the texture is rather like crepe and does not slip. The regular openings make it a good foundation for embroidery.

And let's not forget the fascinating possibilities of double weave.

So far not mentioned is the universal use of twill for clothing. Twill creates firm fabrics with diagonal elasticity conforming nicely to the body. It can be woven in a variety of ways which are described at length in the chapter on clothing design. There are also many possibilities of double weave on a twill threading woven with unbalanced sheds: double widths, tubular, quilted, two-faced textiles.

A lifetime on that theoretical desert island simply isn't enough, especially if you can indulge yourself in hand-dyeing and various kinds of fulling.

In recent years there has been a great increase in interest in multi-harness patterns, and an accompanying rise in the number of books on the subject. I greatly admire the effects that can be obtained by more than four harnesses, but the fact is the more I work on four harnesses the more four-harness ideas keep popping up and demanding that they be worked out.

Unless you have studied rather closely the handbook of requirements for the Certificates of Excellence in Handweaving of the HGA, you may be surprised to learn that no samples in the basic weaving portion call for the use of a loom with more than four harnesses, although you are, of course, at perfect liberty to use them in Part III, which is original research. The committee that wrote the handbook, after much debate, decided that if you have mastered the theory of four harnesses, it is relatively easy to branch out into multi-harness weaves. It was judged unfair to exclude weavers with only four-harness looms from the opportunity to qualify for the certificate.

At a Michigan League conference, Best in Show went to a wall hanging with a large triangular motif. It was much admired, and since the weaver was known for working on a large dobby loom, the assumption was made by her audience that it was a multi-harness piece. Later she confided to me that it was woven on a Dorset which, in case the name is not familiar to you, is a small portable four-harness loom widely used by beginners.

So you need never feel inferior to the owners of multi-harness looms, if yours has only four.

Selvages

It's a safe assumption that one of the first snags you ran into as a beginner was those pesky selvages. Let's assume you have finished your beginning courses and are ready for your first independent project. You have the right type and weight of shuttle, a correctly wound bobbin or pirn, perfectly tensioned warp and a proper relationship between warp, weft and sett. Question: why can't you produce instant perfect selvages, and what's the big deal anyway that the "Old Guard" is so hipped on them?

While it is true that good selvages are a sign of good craftsmanship, there are other sound reasons for working to acquire the skill. In the first place, if the turns of the weft are loose or loopy, the outer edges of the textile will be weak. Secondly, if they are pulled in so they are tight, the outer edges will be too closely woven and will distort the center of the fabric, not to mention the fact that the beater will fray the outer edges. If the fell of the warp curves in toward the beater at the outer edges, you are pulling the weft too tight, though you may not be aware of it until the curves begin to be apparent.

The answer to these problems is discouraging and sometimes beginners would like to ignore it: you need practice. You wouldn't take ten lessons in tennis and proceed at once to Wimbledon. First you must practice strokes over and over until they are consistent, easy, relaxed and produced without thinking.

You have a choice - either you take time to develop the skill, or you can spend your weaving life avoiding projects that require good selvages.

If you are in earnest, don't start out with narrow warps - scarves, runners, place mats and other articles whose edges are seen at close range. And forget about designs with many changes of shuttles. Stick to projects on which the selvages can be hemmed or concealed in the seams, such as pillows, towels or skirt lengths. Better yet, grit your teeth and put on a five-yard warp, at least 20 inches wide, in a smooth, medium fine cotton or linen. Plan a one-shuttle design and weave it off without worrying too much about the selvages. Concentrate instead on throwing the shuttle so that the weft lies at an angle of about 30 degrees, trying for an easy rhythm and consistency of beat. Practice until you find your motions are relaxed and automatic, working faithfully for an hour or more every day. If you haven't the heart to throw away a practice piece, weave dish towels and hem them on four sides. If you should take all this unsought advice (and nobody ever has yet) there will come a happy day when you discover you have been weaving good selvages without thinking about it.

Here are some don'ts:

Don't use a temple or stretcher except for rugs, where they are really necessary. On finer materials you must reposition a temple frequently or it will wreck your piece, and placing it takes considerable skill. Its use will simply delay the acquisition of the knack of weaving good selvages.

Heavy threads in the selvages don't generally work very well either.

Don't try for perfection with a stick shuttle. The Guatemalans can do it, but they start weaving at the age of four and use only narrow warps.

Many weavers maintain that you should weave on a warp tensioned just enough to get a shed, but I have never been able to master this.

Perhaps you might be interested in the methods some of us use for good selvages, with a minimum of draw-in. The warp is very tight. The shuttle is thrown so the weft lies at a 30 degree angle (sometimes called "the weaver's angle.") Before closing the shed, use a finger to draw in the weft from the shuttle side just enough so that the outer end on the point of the angle wiggles a bit. Close the shed and beat. Open the next shed before returning the beater to its back position.

If you observe the progress of the weft as the reed pushes it into place, you will see that it forms little waves running from the wide side of the angle across to the turn of the weft, the final little wave closing neatly around the outside warp end. Watch the narrow end of the triangle and if a weft pulls in, take it out at once by opening the shed and repositioning the weft. If you are using a fine smooth warp and weft, you may want to give the weft a tiny downward pull before the next shot.

The selvages of twills present another problem. Depending on how the outside ends come up in the twill sequence, one or both of the outer selvage ends may not weave in. This can sometimes be corrected by changing the direction of the first shot, or you can drop the floating ends. But sometimes it is best to let an end float, thereafter using the floating end to warn you if you make a mistake in treadling - if the floating end weaves in, you have made a treadling error.

Then there is the good old floating selvage - the outer ends on each side go from reed to back beam without being threaded to a harness. You throw the shuttle first under, then over the floating end. This is not a complete answer when weaving patterned twills or frequent changes of weft - sometimes you come up with three-end floats at the selvage. The place to look for help is Peter Collingwood's book on rugs. His directions are complicated, with such instructions as "Wrap B twice downwards around right selvage thread, then throw from right to left." There is a full page of that sort of thing and only weavers of rugs, where selvages are crucial, need master the principles.

Beat:

Budd Stalnaker says the term "beater" should be changed to "placer," since that is a better description of what it does. In many weaves, the number of shots should exactly balance the number of ends in the sett, and if you are weaving textiles to be heavily fulled it is extremely tricky because the setts are usually so wide. Check the beat frequently by counting the picks per inch. The easiest textile to weave is one with a perfect sett - warp and weft balance with a minimum of effort. It is worth while, on a long project, to sample enough to find the best sett and beat for your yarns.

Probably the most difficult textile to weave is a balanced twill with a strong color or value contrast between warp and weft, because tiny variations in the placement of the weft will show up when the fabric is fulled. Scottish tartans are a real test of your skill, because the squares of brilliant color must be exactly beaten or the patterns will not match when the pieces are put together.

Fringes

There are fewer fringes being woven these days than in the glory days of "ethnic" clothing, but they have their place. Fringes on shawls and scarves are almost a necessity.

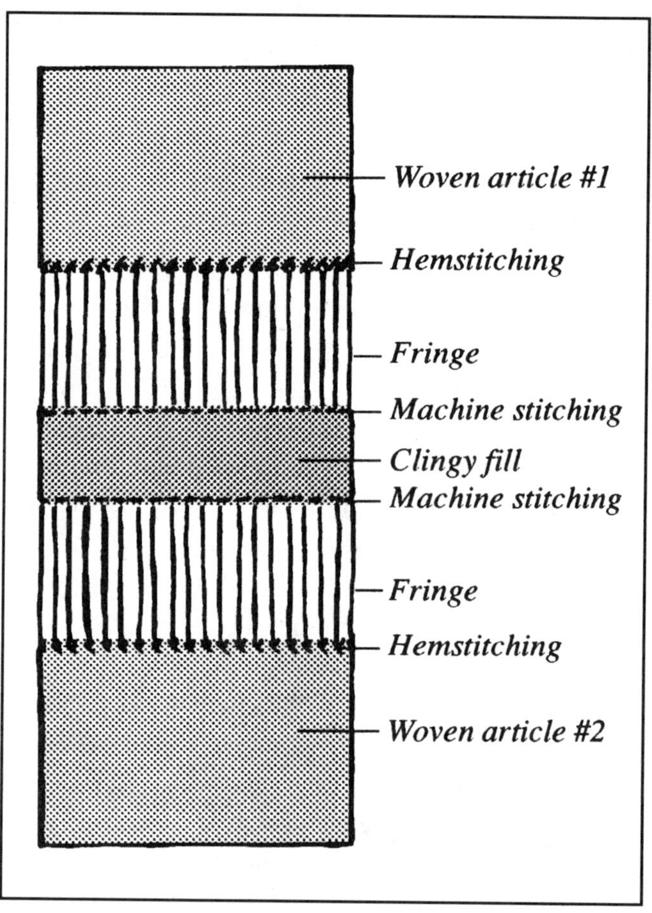

Linen fringes, although often used on towels, place mats and such, are really a very poor solution to the finishing process. Linen fringes are vulnerable to abrasion and don't stand up well to laundering, wearing off and ruining the piece. By the same token, linen fringes on rugs are a no-no because they disappear very quickly under foot traffic, The classic rug finish is a Scandinavian woven edge which ends up in a neat braid on one corner. There are several others that are both handsome and durable which are described in Peter Collingwood's book.

Some novelty yarns make poor fringes because they are composed of one or more fine, strong support yarns holding a more loosely wound wool, cotton, mohair. or other fiber. When you trim the fringe, the large end is, so to speak, turned loose and is longer than the rest of the fringe, and looks stringy. The only solution to this problem is to trim them frequently.

When a fringed piece is taken off the loom, it is not easy to cut it off so that the fringes are perfectly even. Additionally, if the piece is washed after the fringes are cut, a rather unsightly foxtail effect is apt to result, particularly with a wool fringe. A method of avoiding both these problems is to anticipate them, as follows:

For the first fringe, weave about an inch of plain weave in a clingy yarn such as cotton carpet warp. Then put in your spacer for the fringe in the form of sticks or cardboard the width of the piece. Against this, start the body of the article and, after a few shots, hemstitch or overcast the edge. Repeat the process in reverse at the other end of the piece. The drawing shows the fringed end of one textile, the plain weave section and the fringe at the start of the next piece.

When the article comes off the loom, take it to the sewing machine and stitch both sides of the plain-weave area, before fulling. When the piece is dry and pressed, trim off the fringe along the machine stitching. You now have perfectly straight edges on the fringes.

Plain short fringes are probably the best solution for scarves, but if they are long and designed to be a feature of the piece, there are many handsome ways to finish and embellish them. *Finishes in the Ethnic Tradition* by Suzanne Baizerman and Karen Searle is a treasury of ideas for finishing fringes.

If there is a strong contrast in color or value between warp and weft the fringed ends can present strong contrast to the body. This can be modified when the piece is off the loom by tying in some of the weft yarn to soften the contrast.

A standard way to finish articles without fringes or hemming is to darn back the ends into the body, but sometimes this produces a rather clunky edge.You might want to try the following: off the loom, but before washing, darn every other end back into the web. After washing, clip off the undarned ends.

Sample this before applying it to the actual piece. It is not particularly suitable for articles that are going to be washed frequently, but works well on pieces that will be dry cleaned.

SLICK TRICKS

- When your weaving plan calls for two pieces woven side-by-side with two shuttles, as for sleeves, leave them until the last. Weave the first piece with one shuttle, letting the unwoven warp on the other half of the loom run forward onto the cloth beam. When the first piece is finished, cut it off, wind the unwoven warp back onto the warp beam, and weave that half. It may be necessary to adjust the tension by cutting off and retying, but the process saves that pesky handling of two shuttles and the headache of trying to weave four perfect selvages at once.

- If you have always wanted to weave Krokbragd (even if you can't pronounce it) it may surprise you to learn that you do not have to thread your loom to a three-harness point twill; it can just as well be woven on four harnesses threaded 1, 2, 3, 4. Simply change the tie-up so that harness #4 weaves with harness #2, and you can proceed as if you had drafted a three-harness point twill. In other words, if you have a rug warp on your loom threaded to straight draw, you can weave Krokbragd without rethreading.

- Once upon a house tour I saw a beautiful spiral staircase with each step covered in needlepoint - a different floral design on a white ground for each step. (Presumably the house had a contract with a good rug cleaner, or no little kids, or stern discipline.) The idea would he a useful one if you are planning to weave a series of rug samples. Each step could be a development of a single pattern, or woven in related colors. Safety note: smallish rug samples skid easily and would be hazardous on steps; be sure to use non-skid padding and tack the samples down.

- If you want to weave open lace such as Swedish lace or huck or Atwater-Bronson use a hard-spun yarn and a fairly close set to produce the maximum lacy effect. Soft yarns in lace weaves make very interesting textures but not open effects. Even tightly spun yarns do not have a lacy look until laundered.

- In the long run, it is better to tie up your harnesses for the most easily remembered sequence rather than trying to think which foot goes where and when. A straight twill in a heavy yarn, with each pattern shot followed by a tabby, makes a most interesting diagonal weave with an equally interesting, but different, pattern on the reverse. Using a standard tie-up can result in so many mistakes that it is easier to retie the loom for treadling straight across: 12, 13, 23, 24, 34, 13, 14, 24. This takes eight treadles but saves misweaves.

- In taking the weft back to correct an error, there are two possibilities. The easiest way is to cut (carefully) the weft in the center and pull it out from the side, treadling as you go to prevent distorting the warp. The weft is, of course, wasted by this process and it is useful only if your time is more valuable than the weft. The second possibility is more laborious, involving treadling in reverse order and rewinding the weft. This is much easier if you use a ski or stick shuttle on which the weft can he wound as you go, rather than wrestling with the problem of rewinding bobbins as the weft is taken out.

- If you are weaving fluffy mohair or other clingy yarn in an open sett, you will find it easier to work with a tight tension and the harnesses tied up individually in 1, 2, 3, 4 order. For each shot, treadle the combination separately; that is treadle 1 and then add 3. This usually makes it unnecessary to clear the shed with your hands for each shot.

- Incidentally, fluffy mohair yarns are excellent projects for beginners since the sett will necessarily be open and the draft simple because patterns other than color changes are useless. Differences in beat are concealed by the fluffy nature of the yarn.

- When weaving with very fuzzy yarns, it is even acceptable to omit hemstitching or overcasting the edges at the fringe, since the yarn clings to itself.

COLOR IS EVERYTHING

"Color is the best, the most available and the most comfortable aspect of both fashion and environmental design. Color is the first, last and greatest determinant to the purchaser. It is the first thing the consumer and the professional buyer see, and it's the last thing that helps to make the decision."
—Jack Lenor Larson

Many great minds have wrestled with the problems of color, from Goethe to Albers. Physicists have dealt with light, artists with the relationship of color to design, and psychologists with the emotional effects of color. It would take a lot of chutzpah for me to attempt to add anything substantial to the subject. It is possible, however, to make a few practical (I hope) suggestions to fellow flounderers.

There are some books on color theory that will help you. One is a little paperback by Josef Albers called *Interaction of Color.* This is a condensation of his huge masterwork with the same title, which you could scarcely afford to buy but might find (but not borrow) in a big library. The condensed book is used in art classes, and suggests exercises that will help you understand color problems such as the uses of the gray scale, the value of value, and simultaneous contrast (the optical effects of colors on each other). The materials used are paints and colored papers, but workers in colored yarns have better materials right at hand.

The National Institute of Standards and Technology has a publication called *Color - Universal Language and Dictionary of Names.* If you think you know what colors are meant by "rust" and "chartreuse," try looking them up in this one. There are 267 color chips from "Red, Pink" around the color wheel to "Purplish Pink, Purplish Red" with each color defined according to its color mixture. After 34 pages of color theories and diagrams, there is a section labeled "Synonymous and Near Synonymous Color Names with Their Sample Identifications." This takes up 45 pages of color names for the chips, listed in columns showing what they are called in different contexts by different manufacturers. For example, a color chip labeled "Moderate Reddish Brown" has, by rough estimate, 150 terms for its color, most of which are unfamiliar. Just in case this isn't enough, there are 73 pages labeled "Dictionary of Color Names" with about 255 names on each page. The idea seems to have been to provide industry with standards for classifying and naming colors. You get a picture of experts sitting for months trying to reduce these thousands of names to a manageable system corresponding to the color chips. Those must have been lively times at the National Institute of Standards and Technology.

Oddly enough, most of the colors I have produced in dyeing quite closely approximate the color chips, give or take a little. It's a very handy publication for colorists, particularly dyers.

An excellent book, *Color and Fiber,* by Patricia Lambert, Barbara Staepelaere and Mary G.Fry, published in 1986, suggests experiments with direct application to fibers. Like the Albers book, it suggests exercises to help you anticipate the effects of colors on each other. If you followed the exercises, you would do much better in predicting how the colors in a woven design would interact with each other.

Most of us, at one time or another, selected the colors for a project only to find that they didn't look as effective in the finished piece as we had expected.

Here are a few generalizations which might explain why.

1. No color stands on its own, but is much influenced by the colors which surround it. If you add some pink threads to a red warp, the red is likely to subtract its color from the pink, leaving it yellowish or bluish, or even gray. This is called simultaneous contrast, and it is dealt with at length in the Albers book.

2. Values (light and dark) are just as important as the hues, maybe more so.

3. Cay Garrett used to tell her classes that the easiest colors to combine are those shown on one-third of the color wheel (red through purple to blue; blue through green to yellow; yellow through orange to red), and that it takes a real artist to combine color opposites or triads. This is true, though using this approach, and this approach only, can result in rather uninteresting color schemes.

4. Fashion heavily influences our attitude towards color. A few years ago nobody would have dreamed of wearing purple, and today everybody wears it, to the point that it is becoming a cliché. Do you remember when it was considered impossible to wear blue with green?

5. There are no colors that can be described as "ugly." In a dye study group we proceeded with a mathematical rather than a theoretical approach to dyeing, and at every meeting a few colors turned up that were decried as ugly by some or all of us. Taking a firm grip on ourselves, we decided that it was fair to call some colors "yucky," but not ugly. You might find that one of those yucky colors provides just the touch you need to make the other colors sing.

6. We each have our own emotional attitudes toward certain colors. I once served as a show judge with the late Harriet Lynn. She asked in advance to be excused when anything pink turned up, because she hated pink and couldn't be fair. This was incomprehensible to one who loves reds and pinks, all shades, values and tints. Digging deep in my unconscious I have decided, without the assistance of a shrink, that I love pink because of a childhood deprivation - as a redhead I was never allowed to wear it. My brunette sister got to wear red while I was sentenced to green. To this day, if on impulse I buy something in green to wear, it always languishes unworn in my closet.

7. Size of color areas: sometimes the sheer volume of strong colors can create a clashing effect. Big areas of purple and green might look something less than great, but little areas of green on purple, or purple on green can make a lively combination.

8. Unfortunately the general lighting of your workplace heavily influences color. If you are lucky enough to work in natural light, you must face the fact that under artificial light your colors may change. If you know in advance what kind of lighting will be present when a piece is actually used, you might try composing the colors in that type of light. Fluorescent lighting is particularly hard to deal with, but a lot of progress is being made in bringing their light closer to natural sunlight. If you are a dyer working under fluorescent light, it would pay you to investigate these "daylight" fluorescents.

The whole subject of color is a slippery one and there's always something new to learn. It is not much help to be told, "If it looks right, it is right," because if it doesn't look right, what's wrong, and what can you do about it?

Theory is all very well, and the use of paper and paints can help you to understand color theory. When it comes down to it, though, there is nothing like working with our basic materials - colored yarns.

No matter how many times you have been told about warp sequences, you won't appreciate how useful they are to the weaver until you really put some effort into making them. The process is simplicity itself, consisting of yarns wrapped around cardboard.

Last year our clothing study group decided to specialize in color. As a start, each of us agreed to bring in two or three yarns we regarded as impossible to harmonize. Each combination (and some of them were truly awful) was then handed to another member, whose task it was to harmonize them by addition of other colors. The results were amazing, and as the year went on they had a decided influence on our work in color.

A few hours spent winding yarns around cardboard might spare you a disaster, or at least make your work more fun. For this reason, hang on to all your thrums, dye samples and leftovers of yarn and keep them in a big basket or box. When you have a project in mind, take a strip of firm cardboard and wind yarns very solidly in the various colors you think might work. Throw away your inhibitions and theories and try any and all combinations you can muster. Make a lot of them, and don't throw them away – keep them for future reference.

For an actual project you will usually want to start with a background color representing the warp, either because that is what you have or just because you must start somewhere. Wind this yarn solidly over the cardboard and then start adding other colors on top, either wild or mild. When you have put together colors you like, the next thing you have to deal with is the color of the weft – the weaver's problem or joy. Decide whether you want to weave a warp-emphasis or balanced warp and weft. In the latter case you would want colors side by side with equal spacing. If you decide to use warp emphasis, wind a card with the warp color in a larger yarn and the weft in a finer one. When you have chosen the right weft, wind over this base the colors you might use as emphasis or surprise.

The discovery of this trick of winding the basic warp color with different wefts will save you much yarn and also weaving time at the loom, and may even spare you some mistakes. Recently I was winding a series of light and dark browns, on a dark magenta base. One card was set aside and when I looked at it the next day I asked myself, "Where did I get that green yarn?" The color that looked brown by itself became decidedly green when the magenta ground, shall we say, drained the red from it.

This process can be carried to the point where you can reproduce the color changes in an eight-harness double weave on separate squares and mount them together to see what your textile would look like if you were ambitious enough to attempt an eight-harness double weave.

One oddity that will be evident is that bright colors do not look brighter on white ground; they look duller, and are even more dulled on a near-white or ecru ground. For the brightest possible colors in a warp, try a black weft.

An easy way of demonstrating to yourself the theory of simultaneous contrast is to stare at a color for half a minute or so and then look at a white sheet of paper. Your eye will give you the ghost of its color opposite. I am sure that you have looked at two colors, say red and green in full value and found an effect of watery shapes. This is simultaneous contrast at its most unpleasant, but you can use the theory behind it for most pleasant results.

A true gray is quite hard to come by in any material, and to make matters more complicated, a true light gray tends to produce, by simultaneous contrast, the color opposite of the one next to it. Years ago I was in a shop in Albuquerque and fell in love with a striped room-size Navajo rug which I couldn't possibly afford. So I consoled myself by studying the many shades of gray, warm and cool, until it finally dawned on me that the gray was all of one hue and value throughout and the variations were the result of simultaneous contrast.

There are some striking and intricate Indonesian ikats in the Textile Museum in Washington, D.C. One is of red, black and white - that is, looked at at close range. From a distance the eye sees areas of green in the white spaces. So many of these ikats have this very subtle and sophisticated effect that it is surely not accidental.

SLICK TRICKS

- A good color wheel is a big help. Condensed versions can be found at art supply stores. Better yet (and highly recommended for a day's workshop by a study group), you can make a really useful, large color wheel using "Color Aid" papers, also from an art supply store, mounted on black mat board. There are 210 colors in a packet so you have full-value hues of 24 colors. Each hue has five chips of the color mixed with white (tints), twelve hues have their color mixed with black (shades), twelve have color mixed with white and black (tones).

  Working with the chips makes you realize some of the variations on color that are possible, and a completed color wheel makes a stunning large display for your work space besides reminding you that, for example, greens can range from olive to turquoise and pale to dark.

- Color theorists talk about the gray scale as it relates to hues, but it is quite hard to place any given hue in its order of light-to-dark. A help is a strip of cardboard with many gradations of pure gray glued down to it. (Josef Albers recommends that you use clippings from black-and-white advertisements in slick magazines.) Punch a hole in each shade of gray and, if you squint your eyes as you run the card over your color, it seems to disappear when it is surrounded by its equivalent in gray.

- A trick worth knowing is that you can take mounted samples of your yarns to a photocopy shop, where a black-and-white photo will show the differences in light-to-dark values.

- A source of color chips that you might not think of is the paint and wall-paper store, where they have hundreds of small samples of every imaginable color and value except possibly passionate purple. If you are not the type to go in for shoplifting, put on a bold face, tell the proprietor that you are thinking of painting a whole houseful of interiors, and scoop up all the chips your conscience will let you. You may have to change paint stores from time to time.

- We have all heard about a psychological failure known as "writer's block." Seldom mentioned, although real, is "weaver's block." If you are on dead center, not knowing which way to go, try working on a bright red warp. It is exhilarating and always fashionable in clothing.

- The National Institute of Standards & Technology suggests that when comparing colors you place the chips (or in our case, yarn) on a black velvet ground and stand so a north light comes over your shoulder. You will find that black construction paper as a ground will help you distinguish between two closely related colors; this is especially helpful in comparing dye lots.

- Some of the most interesting examples of handweaving can be found in an unlikely place - old films of the Cecil B. de Mille type. No expense was spared. If the script called for textiles they were often handwoven and hand-embroidered. Some of these films can be rented for your VCR, and watched with your hand close to the rewind, pause, and fast-forward buttons. Some of the colors and patterns are magnificent . One film (its name now lost in time) had Charlton Heston looking noble while standing in front of a handsome handwoven curtain at the entrance to a desert tent. And there is a Japanese film on tape called "Gate of Hell" which shows many kimonos in gorgeous colors.

- If you are planning crocheted or knitted edges for garments, you may be confronted with the task of finding a yarn for such trims. The yarns in the piece may be too heavy for knitting or crochet, or using one of the colors for trims may result in too strong an accent. There are various ways of solving the problem, the hardest being shopping around for the right colors. You can use two colors on the needles or crochet hook, but this edging is likely to be too heavy, also. Here is where dyeing comes in handy – dye a finer yarn in two of the colors to be used as one, or blend the colors in an intermediate shade in the dyepot. The use of a warp sequence can help you decide in advance what color you will need for the trim so that it can be dyed with the yarn in the body.

- Black in large areas, particularly in tapestry, can be too strident. Try dark brown and navy in two yarns twisted together. If the values are the same, it will look black, but not dead black.

Design And Fashion

Swings in apparel fashions are so evident that they obscure the fact that there are also fashions in the higher arts.

We travel to Europe to see the great Gothic churches, and it is difficult to comprehend how it could happen that these heart-stopping masterpieces were once considered old hat, even ugly. Coined during Renaissance and Baroque times, the term "Gothic" implied that these buildings were the taste of barbarians. The authorities who didn't allow them to be torn down were probably regarded as skinflints or old fogies who were standing in the way of progress.

The great classic buildings of Roman and Greek architecture, so admired in Renaissance times, were once themselves so little regarded that they were quarried for their marble. If you walk around the Castel Sant' Angelo in Rome, which was built as Hadrian's tomb in late classical times, you will see solid brick walls with holes in them here and there. It takes a little time to realize that the whole enormous structure was once faced with thick slabs of marble held in place by bronze clamps. The citizens of Rome removed the marble slabs to use in making lime or building palaces and pigsties, and melted down the bronze clamps for, presumably, weapons. Who cared about that ugly old eyesore? Even the statues on the parapets were broken up to use as missiles to repel enemies.

The exquisite marbles carved for the Augustan Altar of Peace were found lying face down, having been used as paving stones. Let us be thankful that the carvings were very little weathered, so they can still be seen.

It's unfashionable at the moment to admire Augustan sculpture but all agree that the Parthenon in Athens, even in its ruinous state, is one of the most beautiful buildings in the world. Still and all, in early Christian times a small church was built into it, and later it was used as a powder magazine by the Turks and as a consequence was blown up in a war. Even more interesting, archaeologists working on the foundations around its hill found archaic statues used as filler material when the classic temple was built. (A treasure for handweavers; in the little museum at the Parthenon there are marble statues with some color left on the women's costumes showing that the costumes were decorated with woven bands.)

If we concede that even the greatest art follows fashion to a certain extent, it follows that we can scarcely avoid it in our own work. But the foundation of good design is good craftsmanship. Every designer must deal with some basic considerations at the very outset - weavers are no exception.

The first consideration will probably be the purpose of the piece. If it is your ambition to have your work last a long time, you must consider the craftsmanship and materials of the great Gothic tapestries, whose survival through centuries of use and abuse proves that their materials were extremely durable. They were usually warped in linen (though sometimes in tightly spun wool) and their weft was wool or silk. Linen is highly durable in curtains and is capable of being woven in sheer or very heavy textiles, whereas silk and wool are less durable in sheer forms but quite hardy in heavier textiles. You might consider these traditional materials for your own masterpieces.

The jury is still out on the durability of the new synthetics. (Have you ever seen the Alec Guinness film "The Man in the White Suit"?)

Since clothing is seldom designed to last forever, you must decide which yarns to use, natural or synthetic, each of which has its own advantages and disadvantages. You must consider: should it be long-wearing? Is it warm or cool to wear? Is it color-fast to washing? Does it crease readily and if so do creases hang out?

For rugs you must consider: does the material make a good thick textile that lies flat on the floor, so that it will not trip the unwary? Does it shed soil and can it be cleaned readily?

As a beginning weaver I was asked by a friend to make a bedspread for the the house they were building in Hilton Head. I don't think she ever understood why I refused the commission. Even with the reckless confidence of a beginner, I knew that bedspreads called for design considerations beyond my capability - weight of material, durability, cleaning capability, and presence of children and pets. A colonial coverlet in cotton warp and wool weft would have been an ideal textile, but the traditional designs would have been out of key with a modern resort house, and at that point I didn't know enough to design patterns beyond "Sun-Moon-and-Stars" or "Lee's Surrender." A little later I overcame my inhibitions on the subject of bedspreads by weaving a pair for twin beds in heavy cotton and rayon. It is not an overstatement to say that they were a disaster - heavy and clinging and nearly impossible to spread smoothly over blankets, much too weighty to go into a washing machine, and susceptible to the claws of a pair of comfort-loving dachshunds. (I conned my daughter into taking the bedspreads away to school and thankfully never saw them again. Presumably they had an honorable end in a New England Goodwill store.)

Those of us without formal art training are aware that graduates of art schools have an advantage in that they have learned ways to visualize what they're trying to do. Since weaving is undeniably laborious, we need to devise ways of our own to aid the design process. There are certain tricks that help.

To begin with, you need to have a fairly clear mental picture of what you intend to weave. A good starting point is a series of sketches in black and white. Make a lot of them and pin them up where you can see them. Keep them rough and don't get carried away with details. The size doesn't really matter at this point. Theo Moorman once told a group that she made her initial sketches on the backs of envelopes or scraps of paper, because a sheet of beautiful drawing paper intimidated her.

If you have colors in mind, one of the best mediums for sketches is broken pieces of chalk pastels, working with the flat of the chalk to prevent yourself from getting too involved with details at the start. Students of medieval millefleur tapestries theorize that the cartoons included only the major figures and it was up to the workers at the loom to weave in the tiny animals and flowers in the backgrounds that help to make these designs the magnificent works of art that have come down to us. Make many small sketches in color, and choose the one that appeals to you. If you work in chalk pastels, there is a fixative which keeps the colors from rubbing off.

Verda Elliott teaches her rug workshop students to make their color sketches in pastels on black construction paper, which seems to express the thick texture of rugs better than white smooth drawing paper.

Once you have worked out the colors, you might want to make a full-size sketch, perhaps in black and white with notes as to the colors. If you are weaving a rug, lay this sketch out on the floor to see if it works when viewed from above. If it is a wall hanging, fasten it to a wall and live with it for a while. (Unless it is a tapestry the size of the Sutherland in St. Michael's in Coventry, in which case you'll have to work from a smaller cartoon.)

Some shapes come naturally to weaving - squares, diagonals, and straight lines. Curved shapes are more technically demanding, and circles are very hard to produce even in plain weave. Their difficulty doesn't necessarily qualify them as great art. One entry for a show was turned down by the judges because, although it was woven with two perfect circles – a large one topped by a small one – everyone who saw it immediately said, “Oh, look at the snowman.” The weaver was so involved with the technical problems of weaving circles that she never stepped back to see what the overall design said. A full-scale drawing might have prevented that disaster.

A handy little design tool is the summation curve, first expounded by the great Italian mathematician Leonardo Fibonacci. In 1202 he wrote a book in which he introduced Arabic numerals to the western world, freeing it from awkward Roman numbers, and proposed the Fibonacci Sequence - a series of numbers which are formed by adding the previous two numbers together, as 1,1,2,3,5,8,13,21,34,55,89. Mathematicians since have discovered that the ratio between a Fibonacci number and the next higher number approaches to an ever more exact degree the ratio l:1.618, the Golden Mean which the Greeks used to determine the most pleasing proportions between length and width. Designers use the Fibonacci Sequence to plan proportions, since any two numbers from the series seem to harmonize. This idea is a gold mine when planning spaces in a design.

The weaver designing a piece will find that the Fibonacci Sequence is invaluable in planning numbers of threads or width in stripes. Even such mundane things as table mats and rugs look just right when the length is 1.618 times the width. And maybe we would all look better if we calculated the length of tops in relation to length of skirt or trousers in clothing. For example, when skirts are very short and the measurement from shoulder to waist and waist to hem are equal (1:1) you will find that a tucked-in blouse makes you look very blocky, and a longer tunic or jacket in a relationship of 1:2 or 1:3 looks better. Most of us feel this instinctively.

Finally, when working from sketches, the skill is to make the finished piece look something like your original idea - sometimes it looks much better. A very meticulous warp layout on graph paper can help, if you take into consideration the collapse when tension is removed, and in the case of clothing, its shrinkage in finishing.

A perfect material for cartoons for tapestry, transparencies and other free weaves is ordinary buckram. It cuts easily with scissors and, because it is transparent, it can he laid over your sketch and the main outlines traced. Color changes can he indicated with crayons or color markers.

Since buckram is very seldom woven completely square, it is best to use a T-square to outline the edges. Leave space at each side, and enough at the start to sew the buckram to the heading of the weaving. You will find that your cartoon will roll evenly onto the cloth beam without tearing as paper will, and it won't form creases as much as the non-woven synthetics.

SLICK TRICKS

- A collection of clippings can be very helpful – pictures of things you would like to try or color photographs of natural objects. These tend to pile up in untidy heaps, but if you winnow them now and then, not only will you rid yourself of ideas you have outgrown, but you may be struck by some idea you had forgotten.
- A pocket or purse-size notebook to carry around, is invaluable. Some of your best ideas may occur to you when you are wedged into an airline seat.
- Don't try to put everything you know into one piece.
- If a wall hanging is what you have in mind, please give some thought in advance to the method of hanging. If it is the basic rectangle, it should be hung smoothly from the top, and the bottom should be level and not too ripply. The most common mistake is to use a tent shape with string coming from each end of a dowel. This is a prime cause for rejection in galleries and shows. A much better idea, because it is nearly invisible, is to attach the rectangle to a dowel heavy enough not to sag, and provide a loop of monofilament at each end which can be hung over two small nails in the wall.

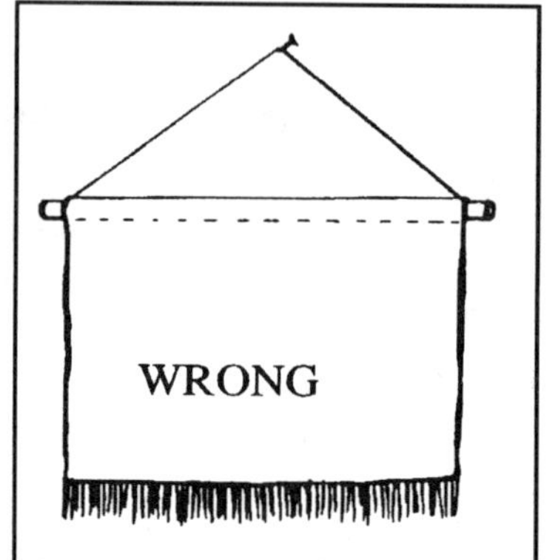

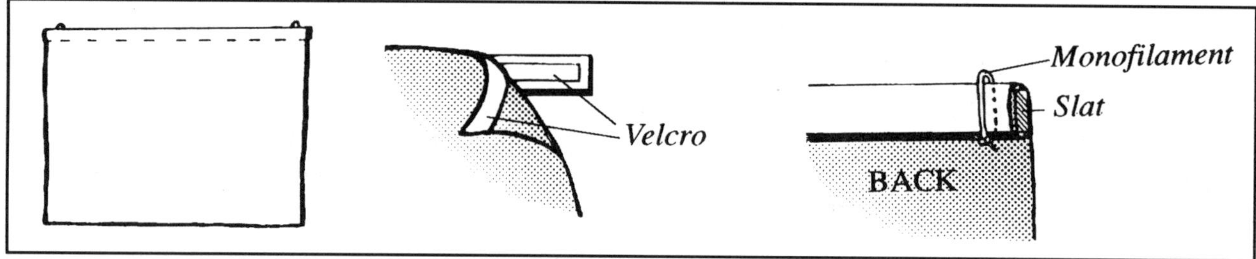

- A standard method of hanging heavy flat tapestries and rugs is to stitch a length of Velcro across the top of the piece. The other half of the Velcro is stapled to a slat which has holes drilled into it to fit over nails in the wall. It is then only necessary to place the slat over the nails and smooth the two Velcro halves together.
- In any case, the stiffening device, whether wood or metal or plastic, should not extend beyond the width of the hanging unless the support is really part of the design.
- Keep it simple. One gallery owner says that when a new hanging comes in with two pages of instructions for hanging it, he returns the piece without unpacking it.
- Sampling: if you are thinking about weaving for sale, your own time is the most expensive ingredient. You may think you don't have time to make samples, but the truth is you don't have time not to. One bitter experience will convince you that a half-day spent in warping and weaving a sample is time far better spent than putting on a warp hoping that it will work, and finding that it won't. Sampling nearly always saves you time and expense in the end, particularly when you're trying out a new idea, color, or fiber. (Of course, if you weave the same design over and over, or work by the book, you don't need samples.)

  There is one catch to the sampling habit – it's possible to enjoy it so much that nothing else gets produced.

- Woven samples deserve to be treated well and kept in a useful form. If they are too large to go into a file, with notes on the project, make cloth labels and stitch them on. The labels are easily made of strips of starched cloth, with the notes typed or written on them.

- Tying new warps to old: warping from the front is a skill that is particularly useful when you can tie the new warp ends to the old in front of the reed and roll them to the warp beam. It saves a good third to a half of the work. Don't do it, however, if you plan to change either sett or pattern, because the changes may be too complicated and the probability of errors too high. And sometimes the knots are too big to go through reed and heddles.

- Occasionally handspinners inquire about the possibility of a "dummy" warp - that is a warp of inexpensive material sleyed, threaded and tied onto the warp beam so that the handspuns can be tied in at the front and rolled to the back. The truth is that there is very little saving, since with or without the dummy warp, the piece can only be woven to the point where the knots are just back of the heddles. The closer the apron on the warp beam comes to the heddles, the greater the potential savings.

- If you are designing patterns either on paper or on the loom, a thing to keep on hand is a square mirror, which will show you what happens if the treadling is reversed.

- Overshot is currently a much-neglected technique with great design possibilities . Try treadling one element of the design over and over, rather than carrying out the full pattern as drawn in. Or use a straight twill tie-up and treadling.

- If you are thinking in terms of a very sheer material, you might like to use fine yarn in an open sett, which is extraordinarily tricky to weave. The ancient Egyptians, in their very hot climate, solved the problem centuries ago, and it's called "dimity" after Damietta. Run heavier or doubled ends at judicious intervals in warp and weft to keep the fine yarns from beating down. That leaves the interspaces quite sheer.

  The so-called lace weaves can weave sheer materials with very little slippage.

- Quote from Louise Pierucci of Carnegie-Mellon: "The eye seeks out that which is the same and that which is different." So if you are making a warp in a random selection of colors or textures or values, be careful that you don't create an obvious balanced stripe in the midst of it, because the eye will see only an obtrusive balanced streak. Conversely, a random-striped area in the middle of a regularly striped textile will stand out like a sore thumb.

Clothing Fashions And Design

In the past ten years or so, handwovens and handknits have become increasingly important in the market. At the outset, handwovens were determinedly "ethnic" – fringes, beads and bells – but nowadays they are more in the mainstream of fashion.

American women have always been semi-independent of the ukases issued by Paris, Milan and London. We are addicted to the sportswear idea, so that even our formal clothes tend to run to mix-and-match tops and skirts and pants. The tendency toward simplicity in cut is a great opportunity for knitters, weavers and surface designers. At the moment we would rather be comfortable than in high fashion.

A question: where do the really long-lasting fashions come from, those we stick to regardless of the high-fashion industry: shirtwaist dresses, tailored pants and skirts, blue jeans, sweatshirts and T-shirts? The truth is, most of them come from the lower depths (from the big-designer point of view).

Pants really took hold during the last round of mini-skirts in the sixties, as an alternative to the short-and-tight mini which is uncomfortable and becoming only to girls under twenty. During the current rage for minis, there is an equal but opposite trend: long full skirts which are especially becoming to the tall (and not necessarily skinny), besides being comfortable and cool or warm, despite the fact that they can be quite hampering when driving a car.

Fashion theory allows for short-term extremes (fads) and long-term swings influenced by basics like economics, life styles and shifting theories about what looks attractive and sexy.

For a long time designers have been trying to convince us that we each stand just under six feet tall and weigh 120 pounds. The real truth is that an average woman's height is about seven times the height of her head. If you apply a ruler to the sketch on a pattern envelope, you will find that the figure shown stands eight to eight-and-a-half times the height of the head; if you are substantially shorter than the picture, your chances of looking like the drawing are remote.

Pattern sketches are conservative. Advertising sketches are even less realistic, working out to more than ten times the height of the head. If you suddenly met a woman who actually looked like that, she'd scare you to death.

There is a school of thought on clothing that anybody can wear anything. Most of the proponents of this point of view, you will notice, are tall and narrow. The short-and-wide know better. If you consider women's fashions now and then to be freakish, take comfort. Think of Chinese women who for centuries had to have crippling bound feet to be considered aristocratically beautiful, and the Japanese women who at one time shaved off their eyebrows and painted on new ones near the hairline. It was also considered chic to blacken the teeth. Western fashion history is not free of such grotesqueries.

Fashionable women in the mid-eighteenth century wore panniers ("baskets") which were skirts pulled out to the side and draped over a reed construction, narrow front-to-back, but eight feet or more side-to-side. Some of them could he folded so that the wearer could lift them up in order to pass through a doorway. (Presumably one sofa to a customer.) Enormous skirts went out of fashion very suddenly with the French Revolution and a back-to-nature fad took over - French women switched to extremely flimsy cotton and silk dresses cut much like a modern nightgown, very low in front and back and sometimes dampened to cling to the figure. Women then adopted voluminous shawls and no wonder, considering life in a chilly climate without central heating. This fashion disappeared to be followed by huge skirts and many petticoats, culminating in the hoop-skirt and bustle.

If you think American women are always more sensible that this list of horrors, just remember the pioneer women who crossed the continent wearing full skirts that dragged in the dust.

Maybe the weirdest of more recent fashions were the hobble skirts of 1910. These were so narrow at the ankle that it was impossible to take more than a three-inch step. To help this mincing effect, some women wore "hobble garters" below the knee, closely connected to prevent long strides. This was at the time of the start of the suffragette movement - women wanted to vote but planned to approach the polls with tiny steps.

One consolation is that when fashions are extreme, the eye eventually adapts to the idiotic aspects, ignores what women actually look like and sees only fashion or unfashion. But let's not be smug - any day a new fashion may come along that is ugly, inconvenient and restrictive - and we'll all fall for it.

Your local library will have a treasury of books on the history of fashion, but the most enlightening treatise on the subject is one that was written in 1899 – Thorstein Veblen's *Theory of the Leisure Class*. It is very hard, not to say exasperating, to read, but persistence and some mental substitution of fads of the present day for those he writes about make it both enlightening and very amusing. Veblen's theory was that all women want to look as if they are so wealthy they never have to do a lick of work, and their men love to see them that way, since it proves they can support useless women. In current terms: long fingernails make us look as if we never had to do anything with our hands; three-inch heels make women appear to be unable to walk anywhere (so call the chauffeured limo); tanned bodies prove that we spend our time on the beaches in the south of France or wherever; blue jeans prove that we live, but not necessarily work, in the country.

As handweavers, we should bear in mind that in clothing nothing is forever, and be delighted that fashions have a relatively short life, so there is room for really far-out color schemes, unusual yarns that are fun to weave, and some of our more fantastic ideas.

Some of us like to design materials for dressmaking, and some of us just want to produce variations on the classic. This dichotomy is apparent in the attitudes to be found in nearly any study group.

Anita Mayer says that she chooses not to know how to follow knitting directions; I choose not to know how to follow a printed pattern.

In the Paris-Seventh Avenue axis the emphasis is on cut and shape. For many handweavers the focal point is the textile, which calls for a simple cut. Put succinctly, if you weave for tailoring and dressmaking you are up against the products of the tailoring experts; if you stick to simple forms you still have a world of possible variations in colors, yarns and textures.

Bonnie Cashin, an American designer who uses handwovens in her clothes, was interviewed by the *New York Times*. Her statement summarizes the credo of the "less-is-more" school of thought. "It's much easier to design a fancy style than a simple one, but I try to avoid it because when it comes to wearing it you really don't want things that are too fussy. All our lives are too complicated to put up with that sort of thing in clothes." This philosophy is for those who like to have clothing they love and wear forever. I have a Bonnie Cashin coat that I bought in a fit of extravagance, and it is now in its l7th year of being My Coat.

At my height and age I prefer that people say, "She looks nice," rather than, "Here comes Faithe got up regardless."

SLICK TRICKS

- If you are planning to use a commercial pattern, select one with the minimum of cut pieces. Bear in mind that nearly all patterns are made for firmer weaves and finishes than handwovens.

- After you have designed a piece of clothing but before you put on the warp, make a muslin pattern. Cut from old material or one from a fabric store, muslins are a must for any design you haven't tried before, even the simplest. But this does not mean real muslin which is much too stiff to give you any idea how a handwoven will look. For judging the drape of any handwoven, the very best material would be an old blanket, either summer cotton or heavier wool, depending on what you're designing. Unfortunately, old blankets are in short supply, though you might find one at your local Goodwill store. Cotton jersey would work, but it's quite hard to handle.

- Anita Mayer's books have several wonderful ideas for garments made up of squares woven on a narrow warp and pieced together. Since she was originally an embroiderer, the surface decorations on her designs are highly original and not copyable, but the basic designs are full of inspiration for joinings, color changes and surface decorations. If the idea of embroidery scares you, remember that you don't need a huge repertory of stitches – master one or two simple ones and use them in creative ways.

  The Bayeux "Tapestry", probably the most famous embroidery ever made, consists of three stitches: laid-and-couched, and outline stitch.

- Double-width weaves: If you have only a narrow loom, it is perfectly feasible to weave two layers which when open create one wide piece. With four harnesses the weave must be tabby; for twills and pattern weaves based on twill you need eight. Double- width weaves are technically a bit tricky to design but effective especially for shawls and their variations.

  The problem of an ugly stripe down the warp at the turn where the weft tends to draw in can be solved by designing in stripes, which anticipates the problem. Use heavy or differently textured ends in the warp at this point and in other places as design emphasis. It is not necessary to place the fold at the exact center; in fact it is better not to. Not only does a difference in width between lower and upper cloth obviate the poor effect of a line down the center, it enables you to see both the lower and the upper selvages as you weave. Judicious padding as the material is wound around the cloth beam may be necessary. Try bubble plastic sheets cut to fit. Two cautions: don't get too fancy with weft color changes, and keep checking by running your hand between the layers now and then as misweaves may join the two together.

- If you plan to weave a garment with a cardigan front or a cut neckline,weave in a fine thread in a strong color contrast down the exact center of the warp to aid in placing them. A similar thread in the weft across the shoulder line will help in placing the sleeves. Caution: put the marker thread in the same shed in the weft, and in the same dent and heddle in the warp as the regular end, or pulling them out will look like a misweave.

- The term "Magic Weave" was used by Cay Garrett for a form of broken twill, treadled 12, 13, 34, 24 on a straight twill; in other words, one shot of 2-end float, one shot of tabby, opposite float, opposite tabby. This weave has the advantage of being flexible like a straight twill but it lacks the strong diagonal line and there is less narrowing in of the width. If you draw this down you will find that structurally it is the same as broken twill (12, 23, 14, 34) turned sideways.

  It is a good construction for clothing.

- All too often miscalculations of the amount of takeup or shrinkage in fulling can result in pieces that are too small for the planned garment. Here are some remedies:

  Substitute blanket stitch or single crochet on the selvages to eliminate the usual seam allowance. If the selvages are not firm enough for this, machine stitch first. Join the pieces with overcasting or decorative embroidery stitches.

  Weave an extra panel for the sides. If you have used all the yarn for the project, redesign to incorporate contrasting panels.

  If a garment is too short, use a woven or knitted decorative panel across the shoulders, or add a band to the bottom.

- Jeanne Treschuk introduced me to this one: If you find crocheting is easier than knitting, it is possible to crochet a band of ribbing to be sewn in place at the bottom of a garment. First figure out how deep you want it and crochet the right number of stitches for the depth. Then use single crochets, and after each turn insert the hook in the back of the preceding row of stitches. This makes a quite heavy but elastic ribbing and has the advantage of being adjustable in length when the band is sewn into place.

- If a knitted waistband is too loose, thread fine elastic through the wrong side, pull up and tie the ends for a snug fit.

- Suggestion by Leslie Burgess: If your decorative band makes too abrupt a line because of difference in color, value or texture, couch over the joining using a fluffy or textured yarn, or in a color with an intermediate value to soften the transition.

  The same idea can be used to disguise an awkward seam.

- If the material is too stiff, use it for the front and back, and add knitted sleeves.

- Sometimes you will find that one or another of these rescue operations will result in garments that are individual rather than routine.

Disasters: Their Cause and Cure

It all depends on what you regard as a disaster, which can range from errors that require a little ingenuity to correct to those that come off the loom so different from your original concept that the kindest thing to do is to give them funeral rites.

Weavers in the early stages of their careers always think that with time and experience they will become experts who never make any bloopers. Not so. It's just that eventually they learn that there are mistakes to come and they can hope that experience will teach them how to pinpoint potential disasters before it is too late to correct the problems.

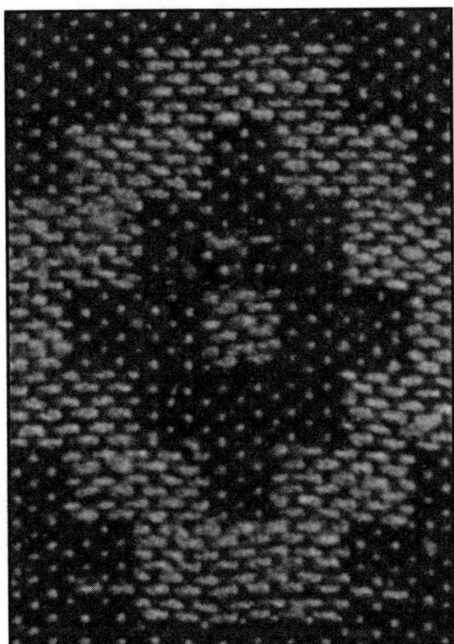

In case you think that you're the only weaver who has made irremediable mistakes here are some stories that may make you feel better.

Over the years when I have encountered outstanding clothing designers I asked each one "What percentage of your designs have you discarded as not good enough?" The replies have been quite consistent: "From a quarter to a third."

A legendary disaster in the history of handweaving involved the filming of a movie epic called "The Robe," which featured Victor Mature carrying a brown garment around Palestine representing "the seamless robe of Christ." It was woven by the late Dorothea Hulse of the Los Angeles area, and at that time was quite a novelty because it was done as a seamless tubular weave with sleeves. She actually made it twice, the second time overnight, because a child in the family cut into the first version after it was off the loom. (Clearly a case of justifiable infanticide.)

I once wove a rug for Lily Mills in a rather elaborate variation of four-harness Summer and Winter which used a complicated tie-up on many treadles. When it was over half done, I thought to look at the reverse side, although the top appeared to be perfect. That's when I found out that one of the treadle hooks had fallen to the floor, and the reverse was a mass of too-long floats. Fortunately the warp was long enough, and there was plenty of weft so that I could start over. Moral: when weaving weft-face (or double weave) either look underneath frequently or install a mirror under your loom.

In the field of dyeing (subhead "Pride Goeth before a Fall") I set out to demonstrate for my sister, who is not a weaver, what brilliant variegated colors you can get with casserole dyeing. I used several ounces of loop wool, a turkey roaster, equal parts of blue and magenta dye, and my trusty Frigidaire oven, which chose that day to blow its thermostat for the first time in fifteen years. Instead of variations on purple, what resulted was brown, as in burnt.

But my personal prize disaster came as a result of haste – a 32-inch wide warp in 20/2 mercerized cotton at 32 ends to the inch. The chain was made just before we left for a vacation trip with the thought that it would be nice to pitch in at the loom after our return. When I started to thread I found I had failed to tie the cross, an idiot's error. (If you think I attempted to thread 1024 ends from a no-cross chain, think again. Some curiosity must have been created when that bundle of yarn turned up at Goodwill.)

Back in the early days of hand-dyeing, a California expert came to the Twin Cities to give a three-day workshop which was billed "for dyeing silk and wool." Some of us had a lot of hoarded silk and that's what we brought. It turned out that the dye used was self-leveling acid, which does not dye silk in the colors we had. We came up with three wasted days, some damaged silk skeins and nothing in the shape of contribution to the group's samples.

Mary Sayler of Grand Rapids was teaching a beginning class, and one of the students was that rarity, a male. When time came to cut off the finished piece, he was so excited that he also cut the cords holding the tie-in rod. He was so mortified that he disappeared and was never heard of again.

Some of the worst disasters come from attempting the impossible (for you). I always avoid strong value differences between warp and weft in plain weave, because my beat is not all that consistent. I once saw a beautiful piece of weaving in fine worsted in a black-and-white check. Beautiful, that is, until the fabric was finished and tiny variations in beat showed up as ugly stripes across the weft.

If you ever come across a "colonial coverlet" for sale, check carefully for the seam down the center. Very wide looms were non-existent and real antiques show this center seam. A Jacquard coverlet with such a center seam came down in our family. There are woven-in letters on the border reading, "Eliza Ann Kissel, 1839" and "D. Arnold, Chambg." This is obviously one of the famed Pennsylvania coverlets. The only problem is that it's the world's ugliest example of its type. You could assume that Eliza Ann supplied the fine wool handspun weft, but she must not have dyed enough of any one color to weave the pattern in its entirety. It is a very large-scale star-and-flower design, and is woven in even bands of rose, navy and green with no relationship to the pattern motifs. If you had woven it, you would have regarded it as a major disaster, but obviously the weaver didn't, since it has been around for 150 years. Family tradition says that there were originally two coverlets - the other was cut up to pad an ironing board. I wish it had survived; it couldn't be any more disastrous than the one which did.

The best antidote for disaster is a study group in the field of your particular interest. Consult them, and ask them to be brutally frank. Out of kindness they will tend to assure you that all is well, but often they have suggestions, such as that a little strategic embroidery will turn your dud, if not into a masterpiece, at least into something acceptable.

When all else fails, the piece is finished and you can't stand it, your non-weaving friends will say, "It's fine. Give it to me." Pay no attention; far better to give a useful piece to stranger than to a friend, or it will turn up in your life at intervals to remind you of your failure. Give it to Goodwill and pray you will never see it again.

Above all, don't let this list of horrors inhibit you from trying ideas that are new and different (for you). If you keep to only what is safe, the fascinating world of weaving ideas will pass you by, and that would be the worst disaster of all.

Some suggestions for avoiding disastrous failures:

Planning the warp: Some weavers advocate putting a yard or two of extra warp on the loom, not only to allow for possible disasters in weaving, but also to have some extra to try out new ideas developed while weaving. Something in my makeup (perhaps my Scottish ancestry) won't allow me to do this, so I have substituted meticulous planning in advance.

You will find in the Appendix a copy of the form I use for planning – use it or modify it to suit your temperament. The form usually winds up being scribbled over with notes, but I find it useful to remind me of what is needed to prevent the project's being short-changed by not having enough warp or weft. The form is filed with a sample of the textile, for future reference.

Pieces too short or too long, or patterns misplaced because of faulty measurements while weaving: If you have designed something with changes of color or pattern in the weft, or different-sized pieces for clothing, make a layout on graph paper, indicating the changes by lines marking every six inches of weaving. (Of course you have to allow for collapse when the tension is removed.) As you weave, you mark off every six inches on the woven web, using Peter Collingwood's idea: prepare a short stick with two notches six inches apart. Lay this stick on the woven selvage, and with a needle insert a short length of coarse yarn at the notches. Tie the ends into a square knot at six inches. When you have woven another six inches – at one foot – tie a single overhand knot. At 18 inches tie another square knot, and at 24 inches, two overhand knots. These are easily distinguished by sight and by feel. When you get to 60 inches (5 feet) tie two overhand knots, one on top of the other, making a nice big bump. Sixty-six inches would be one double knot plus one single. Ten feet (120 inches) would be two double overhand knots, and so on.

Mr. Collingwood recommends measuring with the tension off. However, he weaves rugs which do not stretch under tension. Softer textiles, particularly those to be washed, need a different approach. Measure with normal tension on, and when the piece is taken from the loom it is easy to estimate the amount of collapse when tension is relieved. As a bonus, leave the markers in while the textile is fulled, and you have an easy way to record the amount of both collapse and shrinkage. This is much easier than running a pinned tape, and much more accurate.

Errors in setting up the loom: One error nearly everyone has made is to run the warp directly from the warp beam to the heddles without going around the back beam, with the result that there are no sheds. After you berate yourself for being so dumb, the remedy is simple. You need only substitute a heavy dowel slipped under the warp and tied securely to the back beam.

To avoid errors in threading patterns, try this: mark your draft into groups of ends and above the group write the number of ends on each harness. Then count out the number of heddles you will need for each group and count the number of ends of warp to be threaded. When the ends and heddles don't come out even, you have made a threading mistake, and you need only rethread that group.

Threading heddles is a long job. Figure out some way of raising the harnesses to your eye level when comfortably seated - wedge blocks of wood under the harnesses, or tie them to the top of the castle; in the case of the Macomber loom, just treadle all the harnesses at once and put a couple of sticks under the horses above the castle.

Controlling the beat: A fine end in a contrasting color added to the center warp end will help you to gauge the evenness of the beat - particularly helpful in the cranky business of weaving loosely beaten textiles for heavy fulling.

One of my most valuable tools is a thread counter given me by Irene Wood; it is a magnifier centered over a square exactly one inch each way and marked with spaces an eighth of an inch apart. A fairly frequent check with this will show whether your "feeling" of the beat is correct. I have noticed that when I start work on a section after a hiatus in weaving, I tend to beat more tightly, so I use the thread counter to check. I always post a note on the loom castle to remind me of the beat, and measure frequently.

Avoiding treadling errors: Sooner or later every weaver takes a textile off the loom and hangs it up to see how it looks, only to discover an error that is not detectable at close range – two warp ends where there should be only one, a mistake of one shot in a twill treadling, or an area beaten too hard. It is hazardous to stand on your loom bench to get a distant view during weaving. You might try instead:

1. Looking at the warp through a camera range finder, which is really a diminishing glass, or
2. Installing a mirror on the ceiling over your loom. What do you care what the neighbors think?

Problems with warp tension: Either in single ends or across the warp, these are problems which seem most intractable and the cause of more nervous breakdowns among weavers than any other.

The tie-in at the front of the loom is crucial to even tension. Chances are you were taught to tie in by taking a bout of yarn, pulling it under the tie-in rod, bringing it up and then down around itself and finishing with a half-bow. You adjust the differences in tension by untying and retying the knots until the tension is perfect across the warp, allowing for the fact that when you put the ties in on one bout the tension in others is loosened. This can take hours of fiddling.

Jan Nyquist taught members of the Potomac Craftsmen how to make what I call the Nyquist Tie, and it's much easier and quicker than the old tie.

First you snitch 28-inch lengths of large soft string an inch apart all across the tie-in rod; these are permanent, at least until they wear out.

Divide the warp into one-inch-wide bouts and tension evenly with your fingers. Without releasing the tension, tie a knot in the end of each bout.

Split the warp bouts in two and form a lark's head (snitch knot) with the knot on top.

Pull both ends of the string from the rod through the warp lark's head, pull up and tie a single half knot (like the first part of a square or granny knot). It is unnecessary to finish the knot because as the lark's head in the warp tightens, it will be held tightly against the bulky string.

It is a good idea to start with the rod as close as possible to the breast beam to give yourself enough space to match the tension all across.

After all the strings are in place, adjust the tension of the warp by tightening where necessary.

Test both on an opened shed before the reed, and on a closed shed in back of the reed.

Tension can be adjusted even after a short heading and some of the weaving are started.

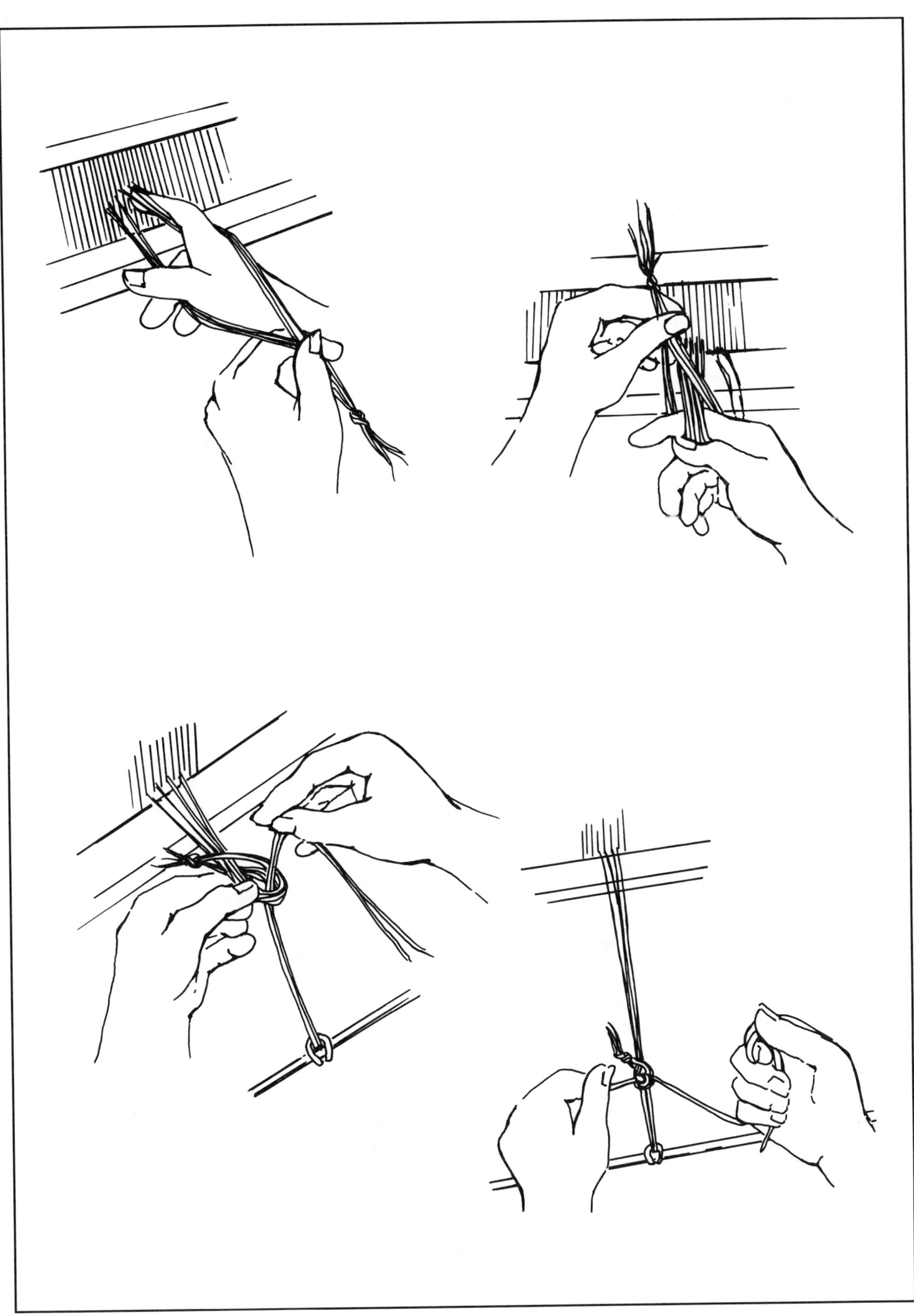

If you discover at the outset of weaving that the tension is impossible, don't, as you value your life, try to wind it forward onto the cloth beam. That will only compound the problem. The simplest way to correct it is to take out the ties to the cloth beam rod and release the brake on the warp beam. Pull the warp forward, allowing it to lie in a loose heap in front of the loom. When the ties are at the back beam, prop open a plain weave shed about 1/2" and rewind the warp by using the methods of the those who warp from-the-front. From the resting position, pull the beater gently forward to the breast beam; this combs the warp. Keeping your hand on the beater, turn the warp beam and allow the beater to travel with the warp. When it touches the castle, stop winding and again move it to the breast beam. Continue winding and, of course, padding the warp beam. If you encounter tangles which stop the forward motion of the reed, stand as far as possible away from the loom and pluck or toss the warp.

The process is surprisingly easy and effective because the ends are already in order. You will find that you have to retie to the cloth beam rod because the differences in tension, now corrected, will have all their unevenness moved to the front of the loom.

If your yarn is wool or a rough texture such as bouclé, or a mixture of textures, no tensioning sticks are necessary, as the friction generated by the warp passing through the heddles creates enough tension, believe it or not.

This is the basic principle of warping from the front, and as you might surmise there are other things to learn about it if you're starting with warp chains. Step-by-step instructions are to be found in Cay Garrett's book *Warping All by Yourself.* The basic theory is that it is unnecessary, in fact undesirable, to have a high tension on the warp as it goes onto the beam - the tension is from the breast beam to the warp beam, not around it. Cay herself taught me the method, and I have been teaching it since 1957. Very seldom has anyone who masters it reverted to warping from the back with someone holding the warp very tightly, which was the method I originally learned.

Peter Collingwood has many suggestions for weavers-in-trouble. One is a way of correcting a tension that grows slack on one side during the progress of the weaving, which usually results from a misplaced padding stick. Hang a strong dowel from the back beam. Attach strong cords to each end of the dowel, bring them forward and tie them to one of the castle uprights. Tighten the cord on the side that is slack. This can be tightened further as you weave.

Sometimes your problem is a few scattered warp ends that are too loose. In the case of selvage ends, Mr. Collingwood suggests "knocking a nail in the back beam" to hold edge ends at an angle. Most American weavers, who cherish their hardwood looms, would find the idea horrifying, and anyway it's not easy to knock a nail into cherry or maple back beams. A good substitute is a finishing nail knocked into a stick which is then temporarily taped to the back beam.

If your problem is the odd loose end, an easy way to solve it is to put a paper clip over the loose thread, bring it down below the back beam, and weight it. The clip and weight will then slide along the loose end as the warp is moved forward and will not require any further attention.

A tight end is a more serious problem and needs a more drastic solution. Clip it in front of the beater, tie a length of substitute warp to it, and pull it through reed and heddle to the back. Darn the front end of the substitute into the woven warp (it won't show) and fasten it to the cloth with a figure-eight around a pin. At the back of the loom, tie the original and substitute warps in a bow knot, tensioning it to match the rest of the warp. when the substitute end has been woven in for some distance, knot the old and the substitute ends together, pull both through heddle and reed, and darn the original into the cloth (again, it won't show).

SLICK TRICKS

- Fine temporary ends in contrasting color and value can be used to delineate the edges of a series of motifs in pick-up patterns.
- If you are weaving a piece on which it is important to know the exact center of the warp (such as placement of the neckline on garments) it makes sense to warp a fine contrast thread down the exact center. This will survive the finishing process and give you a cutting guide.
- If your center guide thread is a light color it could have a further use – measure it carefully over a yardstick and mark yard lengths with a Magic Marker so you can tell how much warp has been woven, and how much is to go. This is for nervous types who worry about having enough warp or weft to finish the project. Using this method I once wove a whole set of placemats the same size – a triumph in my life.

  Caution: do not substitute a guide thread for a regular warp end – sley and thread it in the same dent and heddle as a regular warp thread, or pulling it out will result in a misweave.
- This one is from Janet Stollnitz: Label the top of each harness with a white plastic number from the variety store. Offset each number slightly so they're easy to see as you thread or treadle.
- You might sometime, at your leisure, mark every tenth heddle with fingernail polish. These days you can get many colors in nail polish so that multi-harness weavers could use a different color for heddles on different harnesses.
- If you very often have occasion to add or subtract heddles from the harnesses, put a label on each one showing the number of heddles it contains – saves a lot of counting, but keep the figures up to date.
- If you have a light over the beater, you can see the heddle eyes better if you put a white cardboard underneath to reflect the light upward.
- Checking for a cross between heddle and reed, which is a common threading mistake: before tying in, pick up the warp in sections, hold at tension and treadle both tabbies. If a warp fails to rise, you have probably switched ends so there is a cross.
- Taking up occasional loose ends at the start: After tying in, throw several shots of cotton rug warp without beating, then beat all at once. Loose ends will be held firmly.

- When you are making a warp, keeping track of the count is one of your problems. Chain warpers may find the following helpful:

  Decide in advance how many ends you can group together to shorten the labor of checking. I use 20 ends per group because it is easy to remember, but you might want to use the number of ends to an inch or two in the reed. Count off this set number of ends as you wind the warp, and tie them off. Once this is done, you only have to count the number of groups to check the total, and it is unnecessary to write any numbers down.

  To tie off the groups, use a counting chain. Start with the first group by pulling a loop of string under the warp at the cross and pulling a loop of the doubled end through, crochet fashion. As each group is warped, make another loop in the string. To check the total number of ends in the warp you have only to count the number of groups. If you lose track of the count of the number of ends in a group, you don't have to back-check through the whole warp.

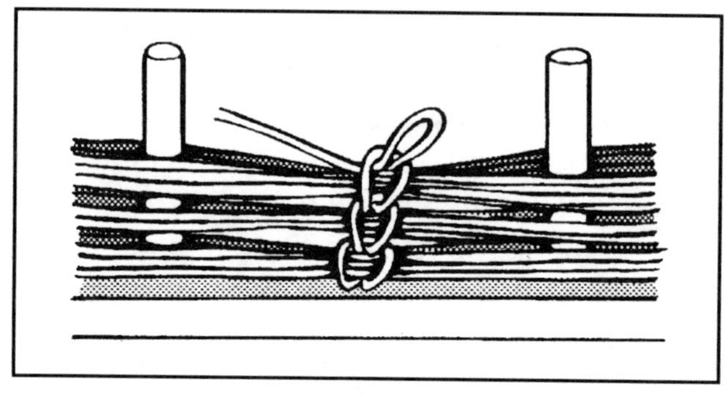

  When the chain is finished, the chained count-string is easily pulled out and a tie to hold the cross is substituted.

  The easiest way to hold the cross is to take a short piece of string down through the center on one side of the cross and up the other, leaving a little space and tying an overhand knot.

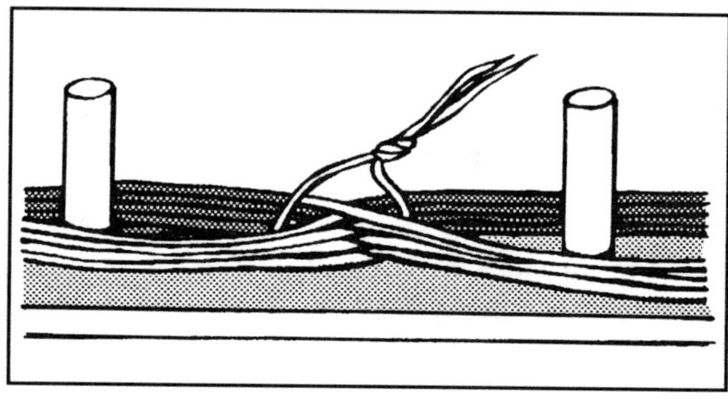

The Casual Dyer I - Yarn Dyeing is a Piece of Cake

"You might just as well say," added the March Hare,
"That 'I like what I get' is the same thing as 'I get what I like.'"
– Lewis Carroll

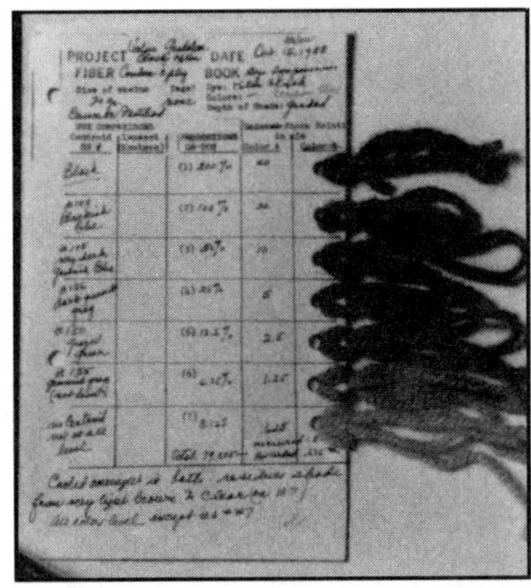

General Discussion of Dyes*

The casual dyer has just as much fun as the expert and usually likes what she gets.

Question: Why dye your own yarn, when the yarn dealers offer so many magnificent colors and textures?

There are several good reasons. To begin with, once you get a handle on simple procedures it's easy to dye your favorite fibers in any color and in the quantities you need. And if you have colors you don't like, you can overdye them nearer to your heart's desire with minimum effort and expense.

Yarn colors, like the colors in any fashion field, are offered in "color ways" determined by general agreement among manufacturers - each season's hues carefully worked out to blend with the predicted fashions of the moment. Like other artists, weavers and knitters simply don't work that way. When purple is "in" they may be thinking of orange or brown or green. Tapestry weavers, particularly, don't want to be stuck with the colors that are provided this season for knitters, and knitters have more exciting ideas for colors than those provided by industry consensus.

We all have our favorite fibers, and when color is one of the main objects it is possible to stock the yarns we like in their natural color and dye the amount, large or small, that we need for a particular project, rather than buying (probably too much of) the color we have in mind.

Besides, if you want mauve or puce, it's much simpler and more fun to stay home and dye the exact shade in the yarn you like than it is to spend your time searching for it. And if you have run out of a particular color and have kept accurate notes, you can make up the deficit with the dyepot.

* All temperatures are given in degrees Farenheit.

A second question is also a fair one: Why not use household dyes available in any drugstore? It's partly a matter of expense. Household dyes are compounded to dye any fiber, and since different fibers take different chemicals, you pour down the sink the chemicals that make up the dye not meant for your particular fiber.

Admittedly there are many fine, ready-mixed colors, but if you want various values, you are in for some rather extensive sampling because the instructions on the packets are quite generalized. Additionally, household dyes are said to fade more than industrial dyes – I wouldn't know.

A third question: why not use "natural" dyes? They are obviously fun, highly thought of by traditionalists, and until recently there was a lot more written material floating around on the subject than on chemical dyes. But I am no gardener or gatherer; the process is very time-consuming, and matching dye lots seems to be a matter of great skill or just luck. Devotees of natural dyes will tell you what they sincerely believe: that natural dyes produce colors that cannot be reproduced with chemical dyes. This is simply not true. An experienced dyer with the five basic chemical colors can match any color produced by the natural dyes.

They have a story in England about a weavers' conference at Galashiels which was addressed by a natural-dyer who asserted that her colors were impossible to reproduce with chemical dyes. A dye chemist in the audience felt challenged, borrowed some of the dyed skeins and gave them to his lab; he turned up a few hours later with exactly matching skeins chemically dyed.

Chemical dyes are inexpensive. An investment of $25 or so in a basic set of colors will keep you happy over the dyepot, loom and needles for a long time. Although the processes of dyeing different fibers vary with their composition, all the dyes are easily obtainable, with instructions for their use.

If you, like this writer, are utterly innocent of any knowledge of chemistry and your math ranges from shaky to nonexistent, you can still become a dyer. As you will see further on, I use a combination of "teaspoon-ounce-quart" measurements with some metrics. This system works for me, but if you are better at math and /or into metrics you will have no trouble translating the basic directions into your own methods.

The pocket calculator has made it all possible for the math ignoramus.

Safety

Before I describe the various dyes, please sit up and pay attention because safety is important.

Some dyes, including natural dyes and their mordants, are poisonous, act as irritants, or cause allergies. You must take care to protect all food preparation areas and, if you can avoid it, do not use your kitchen for dyeing. A laundry room is a better place, or a tub of water and a hot plate in your garage will serve.

Almost all dyes suitable for home use come in the form of powders. For safety and convenience in measuring, the dyer puts these into liquid form, known as a "stock solution." You will be given directions for making stock solutions for self-leveling acid dyes; other dyes in powder form are put into liquid form by similar procedures.

Wear gloves at all times when your hands may come in contact with dyes. You may be expert at working in close-fitting surgeon's gloves, but I find that a pair of ordinary rubber gloves that easily slip on and off are more practical.

WHEN HANDLING DYE POWDERS ALWAYS WEAR A DUST MASK OR, EVEN BETTER, A DUST MIST RESPIRATOR. WEAR WASHABLE CLOTHING.

Work in a draft-free but well-ventilated area. Follow the instructions for handling the powders – if you ever spill any around your dye area you are in for a very chastening experience. Work over dampened newspapers which can be rolled up and discarded before they dry, and clean up spills with damp paper towels.

Pots and other equipment once used for dye should never be used for cooking.

My philosophy about the above is quite simple: most of my time is spent in weaving with dyed yarns, and relatively little in the actual dyeing. Most housewives spend more time every day working with various chemicals without a thought as to their safety, and it is not at all certain that the manufacturers of household chemicals give much thought to their safety, either. But I do take precautions when handling the powders, I don't use dyeing methods which involve sprinkling powders over the yarn, and I clean up carefully after a dye session.

If you intend to do a lot of dyeing, for example, dyeing yarns for sale, you should take safety precautions very seriously.

Self-leveling Acid Dyes on Wool* ("Kiton")

These might be termed "the beginner's dye." The six basic dyes are used only on wool. They are the least expensive to use, the easiest to mix, sample and obtain even results, and have the most complete color range. They provide the most possibilities for fun and games with color, and require only common household chemicals. For these reasons, you will be given rather complete directions on making and measuring stock solutions, sampling and variegated colors. Notes on some of the procedures for other dyes will be given when they differ from those of Kiton dyes.

(Don't let the term "Kiton" bother you. At one time the dye was patented. When the patent ran out, the name continued to be used for a specific dye series – self-leveling acid dyes.)

The five primary colors in this dye – **red, yellow, blue, turquoise and magenta** – will dye wool, and its relatives, to any color in the spectrum. Don't fool yourself that you can mix turquoise by adding yellow to blue, or magenta by adding blue to red. Turquoise and magenta are truly primary colors which cannot be produced by mixing red, yellow and blue. (Oddly enough, turquoise amd magenta mixed produce blue.)

Pre-Metallized and Milling Dyes for Wool and Silk

This is another whole group of acid dyes given different names by manufacturers and dealers - Irgalan, Cibalan, Erio, Telana, Lanaset. They have some advantages over the self-leveling acid dyes, chief among them being that they dye both silk and wool. Many of them can be intermixed. Since the color strikes very quickly and is quite fast, they are popular for variegated or rainbow dyeing in various techniques - casserole, painting, dipping. Because of the quick strike, however, they require special care and different chemicals for level dyeing.

Some of them do not have a magenta or a true red - the reds are scarlet which is on the orange side. The current favorite is Telana (or Lanaset) which includes a beautiful violet and a good black.

* Note on dyeing silk with Kiton self-leveling acid dyes: Some texts list four colors that will dye silk - turquoise, sapphire, lemon yellow and scarlet. The turquoise, and the very similar sapphire, do dye silk in strong values, but experiment shows that lemon yellow and scarlet at 1% to 2% are so light in value as to be nearly useless. Linda Knutson, author of *Synthetic Dyes for Natural Fibers*, states that Kiton colors on silk are not very washfast. For this reason, I would recommend that you do not consider the use of self-leveling acid dyes on silk. I have stock packets of dyes from the past that are plainly labeled Kiton Dyes for Silk and Wool, presumably from the days when silk was nearly unobtainable for the home dyer, and not much research had been done on them.

Fiber Reactive Dyes for Cellulose Fibers and Silk

These dyes, which are relatively new, are especially formulated for application to rayon, cotton, linen and other cellulose fibers, as well as silk on which they work especially well. They use warm water, lots of salt, and washing (or baking) soda instead of acids for fixatives. At the outset they were widely used by artists for surface applications such as batik, and only recently have methods for dyeing yarn been developed. You will find considerable variation in the methods described, but most seem to work all right. Colors are very fast to light and to washing.

Liquid fiber reactives can be kept on the shelf ready to use, have a full color range and are simple to use. Their drawback is that they are quite expensive so they are usually employed for surface design rather than immersion dyeing. They are especially good for variegated colors on cellulose and silk.

Procion MX comes in powder form and has a full range of colors, but stock solutions cannot be stored for long periods, which means that fresh solutions must be prepared from the powders for each dye run. Wool can be dyed with it by using heat and vinegar as a fixative, but the colors tend to be rather light so stronger stock solutions are necessary.

Cibacron F has several advantages: stock solutions can be kept up to a month or more, it uses more water in the dye bath, and it levels with less constant stirring than other fiber reactive dyes. It dyes silk or wool very successfully using vinegar as a fixative, and both silk and cellulose using washing soda. Until recently there was no turquoise.

Linda Knutson recommends that Cibacron F be used with a starting bath temperature of 140 degrees and allowed to cool down as the dyeing proceeds.

Inkodye for Cotton, Linen, Rayon and Silk

This liquid dye is fun to use, though rather expensive. The liquids are nearly colorless and must be sampled as you go. You need no chemicals, just the liquid dye and water. The colors develop in sunlight like Polaroid pictures, so it's easiest to work on a sunny, breezy day. The instructions say it must be used within two years, but I'm using some I've had since 1974 – what do the manufacturers know? The colors are beautiful, but do not come in a really full range. I have not found any directions for use on yarn, so I made up my own.

The Casual Dyer II

Self Leveling Acid Dyes - Kiton On Wool

This section is not for chemists, especially dye chemists. It is intended to help the timid to overcome the fear that dyeing yarn is too complicated to attempt. If it seems simple-minded, remember that the cathedral at Canterbury was planned using a straight-edge and a length of string, or some such simple devices. Some of the directions also apply to other dyes, such as fiber reactive and pre-metallized dyes. Temperatures are given in degrees Fahrenheit.

See Appendix III for a list of supplies and equipment you will need.

Colors

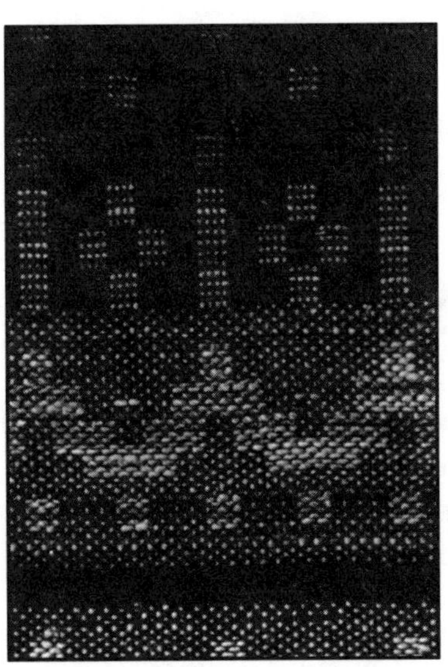

You will need six, one-ounce packages of dye powder, averaging at 1990 prices about $3 per ounce. If you like greens and oranges, better buy two ounces of yellow, which is used in proportionately larger quantities in mixed colors.

There is a handy guide called the "Color Index" which you might want to use in ordering dyes. Most dealers have their own names for these colors but can be persuaded to tell you whether you are getting their closest equivalent to the numbers.

Color	Color Index No.
Yellow	Acid Yellow 17
Red	Acid Red 1
Blue	Acid Blue 45
Magenta	Acid Violet 7
Turquoise	Acid Blue 9
Black	No color index number

Various dealers use different blacks, but most of them are greenish blue when diluted to lighter values. They are very useful when graying other colors, but tilt them toward blue. Mixed with yellow, black makes nice grayed greens.

Kiton dyes are quite fast to light, except turquoise which seems to be a problem in most dye series. They are only moderately fast to washing above 105^0. This is not a great drawback, because wools are not usually subjected to hot-water washing except in first-time heavy fulling, which will lighten the hues almost unnoticeably.

Chemicals

You need only uniodized salt (for leveling) and white vinegar (fixative) which are called "dye assistants". You may substitute Glauber salt if you wish. For the acid you may use diluted Glacial acetic acid 56%, which you can get from a photography supply shop. Use about 1/11 of the amount of vinegar. If you don't mind the expense and you have children in the family, use vinegar, which is theoretically 5% acetic acid. Buy a name brand.

If you are in doubt about the amount of acid to use, get some pH paper. A version with a range from 4.5 (acid) to 7.5 (basic or alkaline) can be bought at any drug store. A better form for dyeing is called "short range pH paper" and can be obtained from your dye dealer; its range is from 3.5 to 6.5. To use, you dip a small length of the paper into the dye bath and by comparison with the colors on the container you will know how acid (or basic) your bath is. Acidity of 4 to 4.5 is right for acid dye. For the most part, a higher acidity will not ruin your yarn but will cause dye to strike quickly with uneven results; much less acidity will cause less-fast color. A confession: I use pH paper mostly when I can't remember whether the acid has been entered into the bath, it not being highly thought-of to taste it.

And maybe chemists know why "basic" is used instead of "alkaline" in chemistry. I just take it as one of those oddities of life.

Kiton dye is adaptable to stunts such as variegated color, is easy to sample, and does not require time-consuming finishing processes. The stock solutions will stand for about a year without much loss of strength.

Making the 1% Stock Solutions

Stock solutions are liquid forms of dye which can be stored and measured with pipettes or syringes for accurate mixing of colors and values.

If you do not have a gram scale or triple beam balance:

Measure three lightly packed level teaspoons of dry powder onto wax paper, pour into a small stainless steel pan or cup, rinse into it the remaining grains from the paper and discard the paper. Add a little water to the cup and mix until smooth, then add about a half-cup of water and one drop of liquid detergent. Place on a burner on low heat and bring to a simmer, stirring until all the grains are dissolved. Pour this into a jar which has been carefully marked at the one-quart level. Rinse the cup into the jar, and add water to the one-quart mark. You are now ready to dye with that color.

The three-teaspoon measurement of dye powder has been used to represent, as closely as possible, 10 grams of dye. An accurate gram scale is quite expensive, more perhaps than the casual dyer wants to spend. However, different colors weigh different amounts. Yellow, black and blue weigh close to 10 grams to the three teaspoons. Red, turquoise and magenta are about 33% lighter in weight, so you might want to use another level teaspoon (total of four) for these three colors. If you do, remember to label the container of the powder to that effect, to remind you to use four teaspoons when making stock solutions of these colors.

The point of all this boils down to: be consistent. As you work you will find that your eye will guide you.

If you do have a gram scale:

You can be quite precise in measuring with a scale. Weigh out 10 grams of dye powder on wax paper, and follow the preceding directions, except that you will fill your stock container with one liter (1,000 ml) of water. This makes slightly more than one quart of stock solution, exactly a 1% solution.

Label all jars with masking tape and an indelible pen, with source of dye, color, percent of solution, and date. Store in a dark place. The colors will keep their strength for six months to a year.

But please note: black and blue dyes tend to precipitate to the bottom of the jar during storage. If there is a coat of residue on the bottom, heat the jar in water and shake until all particles are redissolved. Yellow may develop a layer of mold on top – strain it through a nylon stocking, then heat it to kill the spores. This will not affect the color.

When working with dye powders, always wear a dust mask or, even better, a dust mist respirator. Wear washable clothing.

Preparing the Yarn

Skein your yarn, and tie it loosely in four places, more if you are using fine, tightly twisted, or slippery yarns. Weigh the skeins while dry and tag the information to one of the skein ties. Masking tape with writing in a ball point pen will survive the dyeing process.

For evenly dyed results, it is best to keep skeins fairly small. In wool, they should not be more than four ounces, and two-ounce skeins are better.

Almost all wool yarn from the factory is at least dusty. Dirt or oil used in spinning will cause streaky color, so wash the skeins in dishwashing liquid. Rinse skeins well and leave wet if you are going to dye it at once. If you are starting with clean dry yarn, wet it in plain water for at least 20 minutes.

Preparing the Dye Bath

Water: The standard amount is 2 1/2 pints of water for every ounce of yarn. The amount is not crucial since the dye has a chemical affinity to wool, but there should be enough to allow the skeins to be moved about easily. For pastels, more level results can be obtained by using a lot more water.

Salt: 1 teaspoon of table salt or Glauber's salt for each ounce of yarn. Dissolve well.

Stock Solution: 30 ml of 1% stock solution, total of all hues, produces a full depth of shade on one ounce of yarn. (The choice of 30 ml/oz is purely arbitrary as being an amount easy to divide into fractions; just be consistent.) For lighter colors, use less stock solution, down to about three ml/oz for pastels. However, red and black should be used at about 60 ml of 1% stock/oz, which represents a 2% depth of shade.*

Measuring Stock: Use plastic syringes or pipettes for accuracy. If you are mixing colors, base your figures on the total of all colors. For example 20 ml of yellow and 10 ml of magenta will give you a brilliant orange on one ounce of yarn. Measuring very small quantities of stock solution is easy to do by dilution. For example if you need 1/2 ml of one of the colors, measure 1 ml into a graduate, fill it to any easily divided amount, and use half of the diluted solution, discarding the rest.

The Dyeing Process:

Place the dyepot on the burner, add the salt, dissolve it, add the stock solutions, then the wet yarn and heat slowly, stirring gently but frequently. Raise the temperature slowly to about 165 degrees over low heat, taking about half an hour.

Lift the yarn out and add white vinegar (5% acetic acid) in the amount of one ounce of vinegar for each ounce of yarn. Return the yarn to the bath, and stir for a few minutes. When the bath reaches a temperature of about 180 degrees, check the color of the bath. If it is strong, lift the yarn out and add another ounce of vinegar for each ounce of yarn. Hold the temperature at simmer (180 to 200 degrees) for 45 minutes, stirring now and then. The simmer is necessary for fast color even if the bath color is clear or nearly so.

After the 45-minute simmer, check the bath color – if it is nearly clear run hot tap water into the pot and gradually lower the temperature until it is cool enough to handle. If the bath color is still strong after the simmer, allow the yarn to stand in it to room temperature or even overnight. Rinse thoroughly and wash the skeins gently in liquid detergent. These dyes do not always exhaust the bath.

Spin the wet skeins in the washing machine, but do not tumble. Dry by hanging them over a dowel out of the sun. Do not dry outdoors if there is a strong wind.

If the yarns are twisty, weight the skeins during drying. This is especially true of handspuns.

Tag each skein with a note showing the date, color mixture, type of yarn and any other information you may need.

Some Non-frightening Notes on the Above.

If you can make soup you can dye yarn. Try it. Just take one package of dye, an ounce of yarn, a quart jar, a plastic teaspoon, a 10-ml syringe from the drug store, and a small (non-aluminum) pan you are willing to sacrifice. You will need a timer. You don't need a thermometer if you know what liquid looks like when simmering.

You will need salt, vinegar, and a stick for stirring. Read the sections on making the stock solution, preparing the yarn, amount of water, salt and vinegar, and the cooking. If you've chosen your favorite color (mine is magenta) you'll be an instant dyeing addict.

* Remember: the stock solution percent represents the amount of dye powder in relation to the amount of water used in mixing the dye to a liquid. The percent of stock solution in the bath (depth of shade) represents the amount of the liquid dye in relation to the weight of yarn.

Trouble Shooting

Self-leveling dyes are well-named in that they tend to dye evenly during the simmer. If the yarn is very slightly streaky after drying, however, don't panic; when it is woven or knitted, tiny variations in value may not show at all.

Very uneven color can be made more even by simmering the yarn in a bath of Ivory Snow, or in a bath containing the dyeing amount of Glauber's salt, and the amount of acid used in the dyeing process. This loosens the dye molecules and encourages them to distribute themselves more evenly.

If you want to lighten the color, omit the acid. Even variegated colors can be lightened this way, with very little blending of the colors.

Dyeing Large Quantities

An enamel canning kettle can be used for up to about two pounds of wool in one dye run, but it is very hard to handle big quantities. If large amounts are required for a single project, use two or more dye baths. Very close matching of the separate dye baths can be made by carefully measuring the amount of stock solution needed for the entire dyeing project and then diluting it for the number of baths needed. For example, for three baths dilute the total amount of stock to 600 mls in a graduate and place exactly 200 mls in each bath.

Wool shrinkage is caused by three things: heat, moisture, and friction. Therefore do not stir the bath very vigorously. For the same reasons you should not let the bath come to a full, rolling boil, or dry the yarn in a strong wind, or tumble it in a washer. All these conditions create friction.

Don't change temperature suddenly on your skeins, such as plunging it in cold water from a hot bath. Oddly enough, not much damage results from putting cool skeins into a hot bath, and I have seen dry wool dropped into a boiling bath for purposes of creating uneven color.

With these restrictions, wool is the easiest of all fibers to dye.

You will note that the above notes are all about dyeing yarn, not fleece, because of this writer's lack of experience. However, I do understand that it is done by putting the fleece, very loosely packed, into bags. A spinner can probably fill you in on this.

Quick Sampling

With Kiton dyes it is really not necessary to make a big production out of sampling for color mixtures. A morning spent in a procedure that can only be described as "dunking" can give you a very good idea of which stock solutions make which hues. You will quickly discover that equal proportions of red and yellow do not make true orange, and green is not made of equal amounts of yellow and blue.

The best way to start is by just looking at small dye baths. Add different dyes, drop by drop, to clear water. If you dip the mixture with a white cup, what you see is what you get, as far as hues (color mixtures) are concerned. Of course this will not help you predict values (light-dark). For example, take a purple bath, gradually add drops of yellow and – Kazam! – purple through brown to very grayed golds.

When you have surveyed the possibilities with liquids and found a color mixture you want to try, make yourself several small finger skeins, perhaps made up of several different yarns, topping each with a cap of plastic wrapped tightly with string. These will float in the bath and the cap preserves

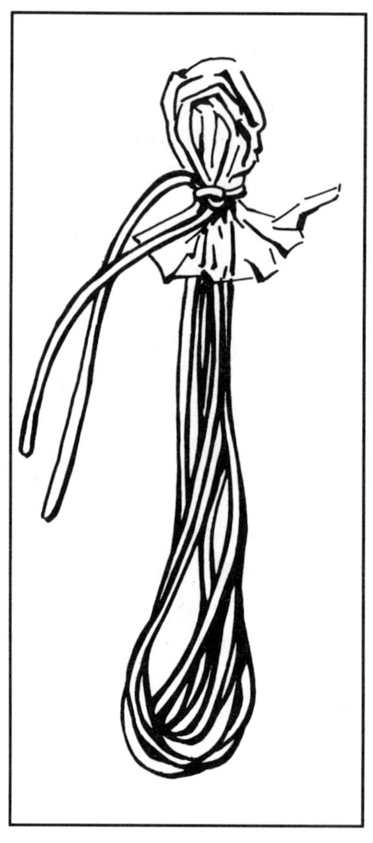

the original color. I call them "float skeins." Wet them out and place them in a fairly strong bath. If you fish them out one at a time as they take the color you will have samples of progressively darker values. Important: This is only a rough approximation of colors because some of the dyes in the mixture will "strike" more quickly than others as the temperature rises, but the process does help to create a ballpark guess. When they are dried and the proportion of colors is recorded, you have a starting point for more exact sampling.

A more accurate way of making samples for hue and value is to be found in Appendices V and VI. You can do seven samples in one dye run, a great saver of time, and your records will tell you what stock solutions to use in what strength.

You will discover from your value gradations on black that in the lighter values, the color is more greenish-blue than black – in fact, some of the best grayed greens result from mixing yellow with black. For this reason, it is better to gray colors with their opposites on the color wheel - that is, if you can figure out what is the exact opposite.

A slick way of working out hues consisting of a mixture of two or more colors is to brush the mixtures directly onto heavy paper (such as the back of greeting cards). When dry this will give you an idea of what mixed with what makes what. It tells you nothing about the value of the colors, but is a good starting point.

In my original dye study group, Cindy Lowther set out to find a mixture of Kiton stock solutions that would lighten out to true grays. Her closest formula was 10 parts of black, 10 parts of yellow and 4 parts of magenta. In a value gradation series this results in very nearly true grays, neither warm nor cool.

Wet-matching is a very important skill to develop. Put your sample in water alongside the dyepot, and keep comparing it with the yarn in the dye. When the skein reaches what you think is right, take it out and put it in a simmering bath of water with the dyeing amount of acid, but no dye or salt. (This is called a "stop bath.") Use this bath for the necessary 45-minute simmer.

If you really need a closely matched yarn color, such as when you run out of weft, matching is fairly tricky but by no means impossible. Recently I ran out of a hand-dyed weft, and reproduced it by wet-matching exactly, amid loud cheers for (and by) me. It meant that I had (A) a very exact record of the original dye formula, or (B) a bright day with good light, or (C) a good eye, or (D) none of the above – just dumb luck.

I'm afraid I have also been known to add stock solutions to an already hot bath when the color didn't quite match what I had in mind. It's a very iffy procedure, involving removing the yarn, dipping out some of the hot bath, adding a drop or so of a stock solution to it, and then stirring the mixture very gradually into the dyepot. If it works, why not?

All this is a bit unorthodox and will be sneered at by really scientific colorists, but it works for me – mostly.

Records

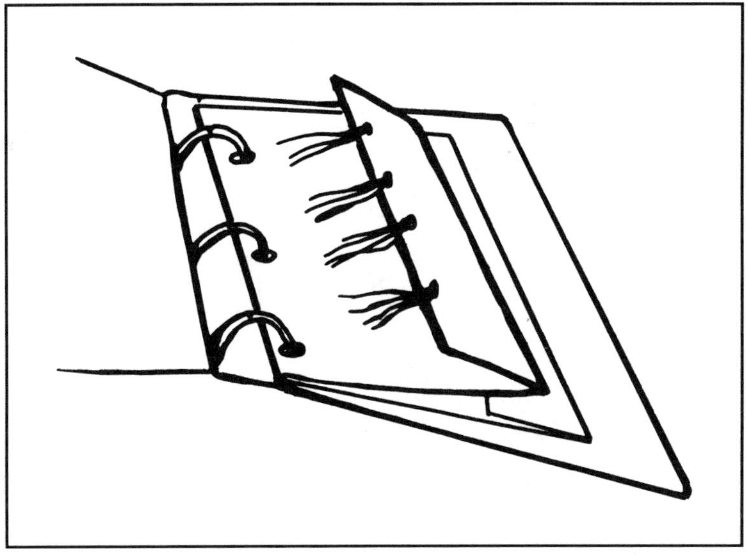

I am sure you have now realized the importance of keeping complete records on anything you dye.

Keep in front of you, near the dyepot, a bound notebook for scribbled, dripped-on, dated logs kept during the dye run. Include comments on what you did, and why you shouldn't have. Transcribe this information into more formal notes, omitting the expletives.

I use sheets of light cardboard punched on the left for a three-hole binder, and with holes along the right side for yarn samples. The information includes date, intended use of the yarn, type of fiber, source, weight of skeins, type of dye and mixtures of stock solutions. Sometimes I add comparison with the National Institute of Standards & Technology chips ("Centroid Colors") and the date of preliminary sampling. I also attach a sample of the undyed yarn. A copy of this form, which you are welcome to reproduce, is in Appendix XII.

After you have finished your project the leftovers can be stored with tags identifying the date of the dye run, which can also serve as a dye-lot number.

If you have read this far, you have perceived that you are going to need lots of color samples. There are some shortcuts to acquiring formulas for mixing colors.

The most expensive, in the short run, is to work from Linda Knutson's two sample books (see the bibliography), one for self-leveling acid dyes and one for Lanaset/Telana, each containing about 400 samples of colors used on wool, plus instructions for dyeing. But if you figure the yarn costs, never mind the time, for 400 colors you will see that it is really a bargain. Figure the costs as follows: the minimum amount of yarn for a reliable sample is 10 grams (about a third of an ounce). Four hundred samples times 10 grams equals 4000 grams of yarn, which comes out to 141 ounces, or 8.8 pounds of wool. If you can find wool at $10 a pound, this adds up to $88.

The least expensive way to acquire samples is to form a study group, which also provides a forum for exchange of ideas and experiences. If you are going to go this route, a logical way to start is by making value gradations of the basic colors – 6 canner baths, 7 samples per bath, resulting in 42 samples. You could then mix each of the primary colors with another primary in a series of hue gradations. Value gradations of the secondary colors would result in approximately 294 samples. The mixtures of the colors with black will give you tertiary colors, sort of, but if you make several series by adding a third primary to the secondaries you will have a lifetime assignment. Don't overlook the possibilities of color opposites, which produce grays and browns.

You really don't need thousands of samples, because as you learn you will educate your eye to the point where you can look at a mixed color and tell yourself it needs a little more, or less, of this or that.

Simplest of all is just dyeing the colors you like, and keeping good records.

SLICK TRICKS

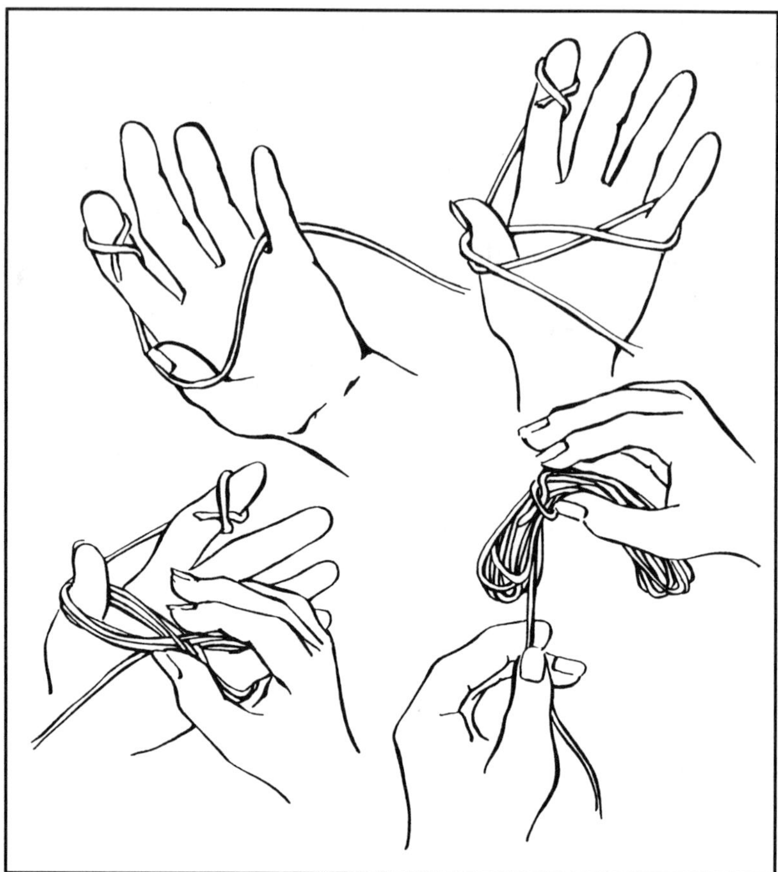

- If you find the directions for making stock solutions and level dyeing a bit intimidating, con a dyer friend into demonstrating them for you. It is much harder to write about with clarity than to do, and not easy to work from printed directions. In my first dyeing experience we had only a ShuttleCraft bulletin by Harriet Tidball to work from, so Irene Wood and I draped her kitchen and ourselves as if we were undertaking brain surgery. We were surprised at how easy it was, and you will be too.
- In general, yarns in their natural colors are easiest to dye, but you can use pastels. The color of the latter affects the final hue of the dye run very little. Don't overlook the usefulness of darker natural wools for grayed colors.

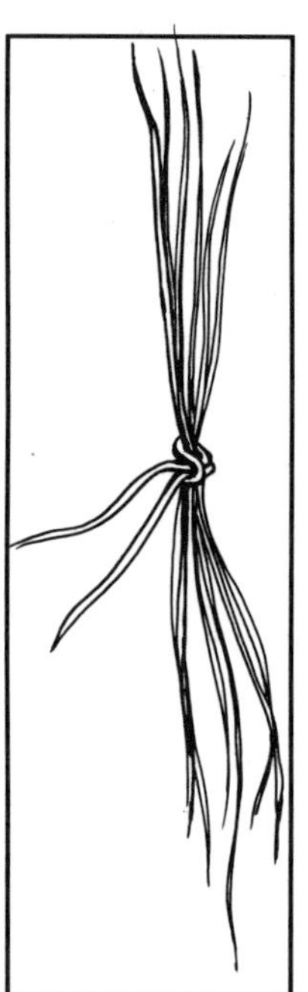

- You will need a lot of skein ties, the easiest to handle being white cotton rug warp. You will save time if you make them wholesale, by wrapping the string around a cardboard, or making "butterflies" over your thumb and little finger and cutting the ends.
- Instead of wrapping and tying a knot over the butterfly, cut the group in two and snitch a long, rather stiff string over the center of the clump. The string can be used to tie the group to something handy to your skeining device. The snitch knot keeps tightening as the little ends are used up.
- Don't use seine twine for skein ties - it shrinks drastically when wet and will create light places in your dyed skein. This characteristic, however, makes it ideal for ikat ties.
- If you are using slick or twisty yarns (silk, rayons, singles wool, handspuns) keep the skeins down to one or two ounces and tie them in at least eight places. The handspuns especially tend to lash back on themselves. The extra time taken for more ties will be more than made up by the time saved in untangling twists.

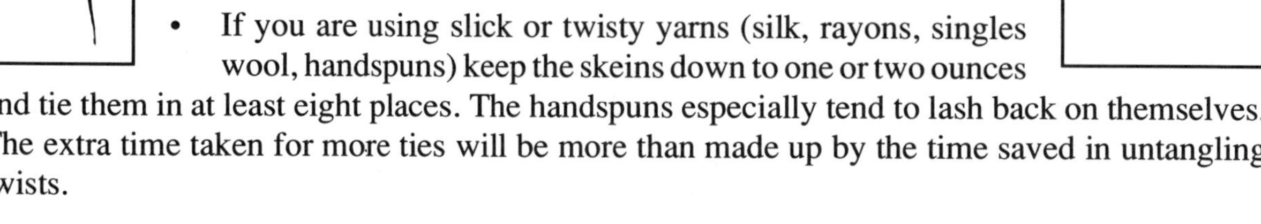

It also helps to weight the skeins while they are being dried.

- Drying is easier if the skeins are placed over dowels so that they can be turned at intervals. Raw wood dowels are apt to develop raised grain which can snag your yarn, so cover them with an adhesive plastic such as Con-Tact.

- Always try to attach "tags" to any skein you are dyeing. These are short lengths of different yarns snitched to the skein ties to show what the effect of that particular bath would be on the tagged yarn. Natural wools in grays and beiges are a fruitful source of dyeing ideas. File with your notes or with the skeins of tagged yarns for future reference.

- There are two ways to check whether your dye run is fast color:

  (1) Tie a short length of the dyed yarn with a length of white yarn, and soak them in detergent to see whether the color transfers.

  (2) Place the dyed sample between two layers of wet white cloth and iron. If the dye is not fast it will stain the cloth.

- If you have a yarn that looks like pure wool, or you suspect there is some synthetic mixed in, dye a few inches in self-leveling acid dye. If after a ten- minute simmer the dye rinses out, the yarn is synthetic. If it is a mixture of wool and synthetic, the latter will show up as undyed flecks. (Sometimes the effect is one of a quite handsome, heathery mixture.)

- Household dyes are extremely useful in matching trims such as netting or lace for finishing garments. For example, "Seams Great" comes only in black and white, but can be dyed to any color so as to be nearly invisible.

- In washing and rinsing, a plunger ("plumber's helper") is invaluable for forcing water gently through the skeins.

- A plastic spaghetti server from the variety store is useful to lift yarn during stirring or for removing from the bath for addition of chemicals.

- A use for self-leveling dyes that you might not suspect is their ability to revive the color of garments made of nylon knit, such as nightgowns and underwear. Just be sure that the dye bath is very, very light, as nylon takes it so strongly, and you don't want to come up with screaming green or whatever. Come to think of it, if you're into dark pantyhose and overstocked with pale beiges, you can convert them into more fashionable colors. Nylon isn't harmed by boiling water. The color will not be particularly fast to washing but can be renewed with very little effort.

The Casual Dyer III
Overdyes and Rainbow Colors – Kiton Dyes on Wool

In their admirable book, *Hands-on Dyeing*, Betsy Blumenthal and Kathryn Kreider state that self-leveling acid dyes are not suitable for overdyeing. This is a surprise to me since, out of ignorance, I have been using Kiton for overdyeing for years, with happy results. The methods described below are also applicable to other acid dyes (Lanaset/Telana, Cibalan, and so on) for silk and wool, allowing for differences in processing.

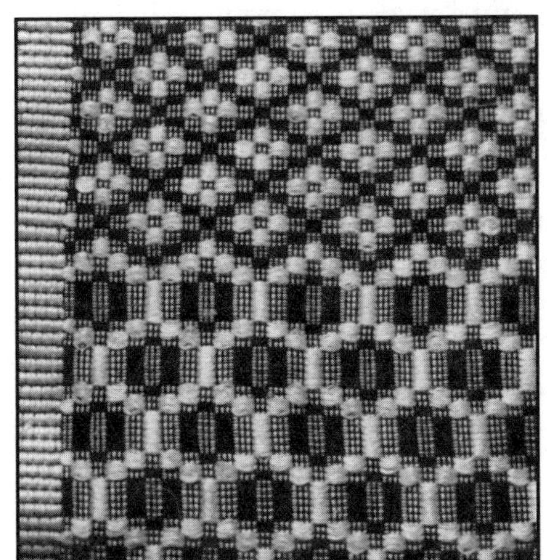

Possession of a dyepot and knowledge of its uses can turn out to be especially valuable when you find yourself stocked with factory dyed yarns (bought on impulse or because they were bargains) that didn't turn out to be such a good purchase.

The first approach is to make lots of little float skeins of these dubious yarns and dunk them in various colors to see what looks best. It is unnecessary to finish the processing completely, as they will be used only for wet-matching. Don't forget to include strands of white yarn to indicate the bath color.

Sometimes you can pick up skeins of nice yarn in several colors – knitting shops are a good source since many of them have a policy of accepting returns of unused skeins which are put on sale at a low price. Once I bought all the CUM 2/7's I could find, ignoring the colors. Several yellows and the hated greens were included. In a fit of experimentalism, I wound all the colors together in float skeins and after a happy morning of dunking came up with overdyed samples - four baths of different colors, in three different values of each: red, magenta, orange and blue. Deciding on a bath of red in a 25% depth of shade, I had enough yarn for a handsome vest in six orangy colors ranging from neutrals (the greens) to really orange (the yellows.)

On another occasion, a few ounces of wool were casserole-dyed yellow and purple, which produced areas of each plus light and dark golds and browns. The results were fairly ugly in the skein, so I divided them into float skeins and overdyed them in series - light and medium values of pink, blue, green and orange. The results were surprisingly lovely and usable. The color theory behind this seems to be that any hue in the overdye will enhance the colors near it on the color wheel and gray the rest so they harmonize.

Sometimes you can overdye a completed garment successfully, particularly if it is a novelty yarn. Once I wove a jacket in a loop wool with a nylon support thread. It came out with the stretchy quality of knitting, and was very successful except that it was green. With some trepidation I decided to dye the whole finished piece black. The overdyeing didn't affect the fit and it came out a nice black-black. Then I discovered that where I had stitched the cut edges before applying the crocheted bands I had used light green cotton-poly thread which didn't take the dye at all. The answer to this ugly effect was on my desk: a black Magic Marker which I used to dot the places where the light stitching showed. Of course for the lifetime of the garment it may have to be, so to speak, re-Magic Markered when the light stitching pops into view.

Warning: before you try overdyeing a deep color on a completed garment in novelty yarn, be sure the support thread is nylon, which takes acid dyes, not other synthetics which do not, although light or pastel overdyes will not look too terrible. Dyeing a finished piece woven of plain wool, rather than novelty yarn, might result in over-fulling and shrinkage. Don't try it unless you are in a what-have-I-got-to-lose frame of mind.

Variegated or Rainbow Dyeing

From time to time I teach a workshop for beginning dyers at a local weaving center. Lately it seems that the natives are growing restless. They are disappointed at being taught level dyeing; what they want are instructions on how to create multicolored yarns. I try to keep their noses to the grindstone on the theory that sooner or later they will want to know how to produce even color - either variegated yarns will go out of fashion or they will want to knit or weave something in a plain color.

Actually, for playing with variegated color, first you need to know what the rules are for level color, and then decide how to break them.

These methods produce level color	These methods produce uneven color
Dye that is easy to level (Kiton)	Dye that is hard to level
Loose skein ties	Tight skein ties (this is ikat)
Salt to slow the strike of the dye	No salt
Stock solutions well mixed in the bath	Stock solutions unevenly distributed
Lots of stirring	No stirring
Lots of water	Very little water
Acid based on weight of the yarn	Overacid bath
Slow heating	Quick heating

Casserole Dyeing (lots of acid, no salt, no stirring; quick heating)

This method, which was one of the first pioneered by hand dyers, has a lot to offer to the experimental-minded. It is quick, easy to do, and above all produces very few of the patterned repeats you may encounter in factory-dyed, variegated yarns.

It is not a good idea to use your kitchen microwavee for casserole dyeing. The microwave oven is lined with plastic which may absorb the dye and contaminate food.

There are some disadvantages: lack of complete control, limited amount of yarn you can dye in one run (even in a large oven container), and the near- impossibility of exactly repeating a dye run. For the latter reason, if you are dyeing a lot of yarn for a project, it is best to use two baths, one for the warp and one for the weft, matching procedures as closely as possible. Incidentally, variegated yarn in both warp and weft produces some wonderful effects, sort of a disappearing plaid.

Here is the basic procedure. Starting with dry clean yarn, just cover it with water mixed with vinegar in the proportion of one ounce of vinegar to an ounce of yarn. Let it stand 30 minutes. Drain it and place in an oven container with a lid – a turkey roaster is perfect because it has a large flat area. Preheat the oven to 350 degrees.

Put the stock solutions in squeeze bottles, dilute them according to the values you have in mind (here is where creativity comes in), and squeeze color in patches over the skeins. Place the pot in the oven, cover and cook it for 20 minutes. Then pour boiling water over the yarn, just enough to cover it, and cook for 30 minutes. Cool, rinse, and wash.

Some observations on the colors: two colors of stock solutions will produce A in lights and darks, B in lights and darks, and AB in lights and darks. (Blue and magenta will produce pale to deep blue, bright magenta to pinks, and various values of lavender and purple.) Three colors of stock solutions will result in A, B and C in darks and lights, plus AB, AC, BC, and ABC in different values. You may find that if you are using several hues, the dark values look best.

The bath will generally completely exhaust and the colors will be quite strong even if you use a total of all colors of about 20 ml of stock solution for each ounce of yarn.

If you are using Kiton dyes, the boiling water tends to level and blend the colors, so generally you won't get white areas. If you use pre-metallized dyes the effects will be less blended.

An experimental, not to say free-wheeling attitude can come up with interesting variations on the original approach. For instance, if you want stronger, less blended color, use a stronger vinegar solution (vinegar seems to he harmless to wool). Apply your colors less diluted and rinse the skeins in very hot water after the first 20 minutes, before adding the boiling water. Or you could include vinegar in the last application of boiling water, thus preventing the self-leveling effect. You will be able to judge which method to use when you have surveyed what happened in the first heating.

For pastels, cut way down on the ratio of stock solutions to the weight of the yarn (depth of shade) and apply very diluted.

For more blending and less contrast, drain the yarn well before applying color, or even squeeze it gently, which promotes wicking from one area to another. Scatter applications of stock solutions over small areas and overlap colors.

For graying all colors, include a very small amount of black or brown stock solution mixed into the final boiling water.

For more general all-over color, either add color to the boiling water or dye the skeins to a light value of one color in advance.

Before you judge the results, reskein or ball the yarn when it is dry so the colors mix.

Disasters can be leveled, lightened or overdyed.

Casserole dyeing has two great disadvantages – it works only on limited quantities of yarn, and small samples are not much help.

The process is not for the timid, but it's fun and very creative.

Dip Dyeing (no salt, lots of acid, no stirring, quick heating)

The most casual form of variegated dyeing depends on your eye to a great extent, and consists of holding one end of a skein in the dyepot (without salt) until it is dark enough to please you, then dipping the other end, allowing the colors to overlap. The skeins can be folded and held with rubber bands so that knobs can be dipped in different colors.

When all of the colors have been applied, place the skein in a stop bath (which is the name for water with the dyeing amount of acid but no stock solution or salt) for the necessary 45-minute simmer. The bath should be hot when the yarn is entered.

To prove that there is nothing new under the sun, my first experiments with this technique date back twenty years, when a friend gave me a book published in 1928, on dyeing. The author suggested that you dip part of the yarn for a scarf or sweater in violet, part in orange, and then finish by simmering in red. The process is a bit messy to handle and depends heavily on your eye to prevent one color from being of darker value than the rest, but it turns out some pretty wild reds. For this reason it is best not to use a very strong concentration of any one color in the successive baths. It uses one-third of the color wheel, so it could be successful in a range of purple through blue to green, or orange through yellow to green.

One problem with dip-dyes is that they tend to create decided patterns on the finished piece, which you may or may not like. Consequently a narrow knitted or woven area, such as a sleeve or ribbed bands, may have a different pattern from the wider areas such as the body. This happens in weaving when you narrow the warp for sleeves or use two shuttles for neck or front openings. It is better to weave all the pieces the same width and rely on cutting.

Painting (strong fixative, steaming instead of simmering, no salt, quick heating)

You will need a steamer for this, such as a canner with its rack turned upside down. There may be a certain pleasant amount of pattern in painted warp chains or weft skeins.

You will need strong stock solutions (2% to 4%) for dark colors, and if you are using mixed stock solutions, provide for extra amounts to allow for waste in application.

Wet out the yarn in a solution of one ounce of vinegar to one quart of water. After 30 minutes, spin out the liquid. Lay the yarn out on a table covered with newspapers topped by sheets of plastic wrap. Put stock solutions in small containers, diluted according to the values you are trying for, and apply them with syringes or sponge paint brushes. If you do not want the colors to overlap, leave a little white space between them. Keep paper towels at hand to blot up excess dye, and check to see that no undyed areas are left on the bottom of the skeins. Roll them loosely in plastic wrap, separating the color areas as best you can. Place them snaked around on the rack of the canner over a couple of inches of boiling water. Steam for about 20 minutes for wool, 10 minutes for mohair.

Another possibility is to include the acid in the stock solutions.

It is possible to make color and value gradations by this method if you leave quite a bit of space between the different gradations. For value, dilute the stock by measured amounts in a series of small containers. For color use different proportions of stock solutions in graded series – label each container and keep very careful notes so you can reproduce the results in larger projects.

Painting makes it possible to control the distribution of the colors better than with casserole or dip-dyeing – what you see is what you get.

Janet Stollnitz uses long warps for a series of silk scarves, tying off the scarf lengths to keep the dyes from overlapping. She then paints Lanaset/Telana stocks in different colors on each scarf section, generally using strong values and grayed colors, which she weaves with dark plain wefts for warp emphasis.

Ikat (tight ties)

This is the most demanding of all dye methods and has a long tradition in the Orient and Latin America, where the usual fibers are silk or cotton which do not stretch as does wool. Although patterns are possible in wool, there are other uses for the technique besides pattern.

For patterned ikat, the warp and/or weft are tensioned and then tied very tightly with string or tape in pre-planned areas so that when the skeins are immersed in the dye-bath the color cannot penetrate the tied areas. By adjustment on the loom it is possible to have intricate pattern repeats, which of course requires a great deal of skill. Patterns tend to be traditional. In fact, in Guatemala the patterns are so traditional that in the markets you can buy cotton ikat-dyed warps prepared by specialists.

Wool is much trickier to dye into patterns because of its stretch under tension. An Australian dyer once told me that if you soak the dyed warp in thinned liquid starch with a few drops of baby oil, when dried it will not stretch the pattern out of register. This information is passed on to you for what it is worth – I have not tried it.

Most of us have heard about the silk weavers in Japan who have their fingernails filed into grooves for "beating" the weft. Weavers in Kyoto working on weft ikat, have their fingernails filed for the purpose of gently bubbling the weft patterns into place – the actual beating done with a reeded beater as in our looms.

The Japanese are expert in making their ikat ties with a plastic tape, wrapping it around long stretches of yarn and employing a knot at the end which is capable of being pulled out without cutting. This takes quite a lot of practice. My method is simpler, for me; I wrap and tie balloons for short areas, and longer reserved areas are enclosed in plastic wrap carefully folded to exclude dye. Over the plastic are tight ties at each end in seine twine. The long areas of plastic are then wrapped with string because, as the bath heats, the plastic may swell and wick the unwanted color under the ties. Leaving the yarn in a cooling bath will also wick color under the ties.

By using ikat techniques, it is possible to get fascinating random-color dashes and dots rather than patterns. For example, make as long a skein as possible, pick up small areas at random and wrap tightly, then dye the skein medium blue. Dry, re-tension the skein, remove some of the first ties and tie other areas to reserve the blue. If the skein is then dyed magenta, the yarn will have a purple ground with random dots and dashes of magenta, blue, and white. If you are working on such a plan, you must think in terms of the color of the background which has to be a secondary or tertiary hue. In other words, think the way batikers and watercolorists do.

Rubber bands, however tight, do not work for ikat.

Slick Tricks

There are wilder ideas for getting variegated color:

- At the Michigan League there was a demonstration fit to curl a dyer's hair. Starting with a clear, boiling acid bath, the yarn was dropped in dry, and the colors were poured over. The heat was turned down and the pot was simmered without stirring. The yarn didn't seem to be harmed in the least. For this you need a tall narrow pot and the courage of your convictions.
- You can tie your skeins in knots and simmer in the pot. After rinsing and washing, loosen some knots and re-tie in other places for immersion in baths of another color. Long skinny skeins would be best for this.
- You can wind your yarn into loose balls, tie string around them and drop them in a dye bath. Or you can squirt stock solutions into them with syringes. The latter should be processed with steaming. The acid fixative could be in a pre-soak of the yarn, or included with the stock solutions.
- You can wet out the skeins in acid solution and spin them in the washer; spread them out over a dowel and spray them with color. This produces flecks and dots.
- You can even dye wool with Kool Aid, which is logical since the drink is made of dye and acid (you won't need the sugar). Children enjoy this method, and it's safe for them.
- Or you can dream up your own techniques. I have experimented with cotton string soaked in strong stock solutions of acid dyes and dried. When tied around white yarn, squirted with vinegar solution and covered with plastic wrap, steaming produces white yarn with dashes of color.

  Some of my ideas haven't worked out very well but were interesting to try.
- Long skeins, not too thick, are better for rainbow dyeing, so use your skeiner at its maximum extension, or make skeins on a warping mill or board.
- For handwovens, short dashes of variegated colors can be successful because the color streaks are stretched out; the same yarn knitted or crocheted could be quite spotty-looking, so longer dashes of color are more successful.
- You can use a card-wound warp sequence to check the effect of warp emphasis. The overall color can be checked by crocheted or knitted swatches.
- Painted skeins or warps can be fairly tricky and messy to handle, and one hazard is that you might fail to get the dye through the bottom of the skein, which results in unpleasant white spots. One way to avoid this is to include in the fixative pre-soak a few drops of the dominant color, so the spots are at least pastel, not white. (If you are applying dark colors, you will just have to be more careful.)

The Casual Dyer IV Dyes for Silk, Cellulose and Protein Fibers

Most of this writer's experience has been with the self-leveling acid dyes, so these notes are only included for the purpose of encouraging you to investigate the possibilities of dyes other than Kiton, particularly for dyeing silk and cellulose fibers.

Perhaps this is the point to mention the dyeing of fibers we usually refer to as synthetics: acetate, triacetate, polyester, nylon and plastic - generally known to the consumer as Dacron, Kodel, Fortrel, Quiana nylon, nylon spandex and so on. The dyeing texts have no information on home dyeing for anything except nylon, which dyes with acid dyes. The Cerulean Blue catalog has information on disperse dyes, which apparently dye these synthetics, but are not widely used by home dyers.

Your dye source will supply you with general instructions on the use of the types discussed below.

One problem you will run into is that different names are used for the same colors. Sometimes what is called "magenta" is really fuschia, and the reverse. I have an acid dye of unknown source of a color called "rubine" which turns out to be a true magenta. Since it dyes both silk and wool with level results, there is more than a suspicion that it is Benzyl, which was phased out years ago because it was considered to be carcinogenic. Too bad. It was easy to level and brilliant on silk.

Pre-Metallized Dyes for Both Silk and Wool:

There are several of these which go by a bewildering number of names which change from time to time. Principal among them at the moment is a Ciba dye which started out being called Lanaset but is now known in some quarters as Telana. These dyes share several characteristics – they dye both wool and silk, and they can be used for level dyeing by immersion, but they require different acids than Kiton dyes, and require more skill and care for even results. Because they strike very quickly, they are ideal for methods aimed at rainbow or variegated results.

Using Lanaset/Telana as an example:

The colors in this series do not constitute a complete range since there is no true magenta. The color listed as magenta is really a grayed, purplish red. There is also no equivalent to the Kiton Acid Red 1. The Lanaset/Telana red is scarlet, which is on the orange side; as a consequence the dyer finds that some hues are not possible. This is offset by a brilliant violet and a black that lightens into true grays.

Producing level colors requires more precise methods than the self-leveling acids – closer measuring and monitoring the temperature and acidity of the bath. Three chemicals are used: Glauber's salt, 56% glacial acetic acid, and sodium acetate.

Stock solutions are usually made at 2% (20 grams of dye powder to one liter of water; in teaspoon terms this would be six level teaspoons to one quart of water). By this you can assume that the dye is less strong than Kiton; this is offset by the fact that the baths are usually completely exhausted.

I see no reason why the more casual methods of sampling hues used for Kiton should not work for this dye series, since level results are not a concern. The processes of dip-dyeing, casserole dyeing, and painting-plus-steaming are ideal, because all you need is glacial acetic acid and heat.

Value gradations can be made by painting the progressively diluted stocks on a skein which has been treated with acid. You need an acidity of 4 to 4.5 pH. For hue gradation you make up cups of dye mixtures (making careful records of the mixtures used) paint them on in a series, and steam - 20 minutes for wool, 15 for silk.

Casserole, dip and ikat dyeing would be the same as described for Kiton, but would probably be easier because you do not have to protect the colors from the leveling tendencies of Kiton.

Fiber Reactive Dyes for Cellulose Fibers, Silk and Wool

Fiber reactives are a recently developed form of dye and have the great advantage of being very fast both to light and to washing.

If you look into different texts on the subject, however, you will find that there are varying directions for their use, most of them being based on the processes of direct application to fabric, not yarn. I can only quote Kipling –

> There are nine and sixty ways of constructing tribal lays,
> And every single one of them is right!

The best advice I can offer is that you pick a process that works for you, and stick to it.

These dyes are for use on cellulose fibers and silk with washing soda (sodium carbonate) as a fixative, and for silk and wool with acid and heat as a fixative. Silk does well with either soda or vinegar, so you can use whichever is easier for you. They come with many different names and usually with a full range of color. Whatever you buy, be sure to get specific directions for their use. For purposes of discussion, the following is a brief survey of the ones most frequently used.

Fiber reactive dyes have some advantages over the acid-based dyes for wool, and are standard for use on cellulose and silk. The various types intermix well with others in the series. The different series, however, do not mix with each other.

There are also some disadvantages to fiber reactives. There is no possibility of free-wheeling sampling of color by dunking methods, because colors do not stay in the fiber until the rather long process of dyeing is completed. You can overcome this problem as far as hues are concerned by mixing colors and painting the dye full strength on water color or other good paper – pure white blotters work, too. This is not much help when you want to determine values.

Another drawback is that much of the dye goes into the bath, which means that you must use a specified amount of water, usually 20 or 30 times the weight of the fiber. This low-water ratio makes it hard to level the color and requires much stirring, plus laborious washing and rinsing.

The work really begins when it is time to rinse the finished fibers. You need huge quantities of water and rather stern measures such as boiling in Synthrapol or washing and rinsing in hot water in the washing machine, neither being great for silk and wool yarns, but no problem for cottons, linens and rayons.

Fiber reactives take a great deal of salt – from 50% of the weight of the fiber for light to medium values to 120% for dark values, which complicates sampling. Since I am a casual dyer, I find it easiest to stick to one percentage of salt, arbitrarily selected as 100% of the weight of fiber, which comes under the head of selecting a procedure and sticking to it.

For variegated effects, there is no equivalent to dip-dyeing which works with acid dyes. What you have left is casserole dyes on silk and wool, and painting and batching* for cellulose and silk with soda as fixative.

From most dye distributors you have a choice of three fiber reactives: Procion H Liquid, Procion MX (powder), and Cibacron F (powder).

Liquid Procion comes in bottles of liquid concentrate which you dilute with water and urea to make a stock solution of 1%. Both liquid dye and stock solution have a long shelf life, and you do not have the problem of turning powdered dyes into liquid form with attendant dust masks and other precautions. It dyes cellulose fibers, silk, and wool, has a complete color range and can be ordered in kit form for experiments. It is relatively expensive and therefore not much used for immersion dyeing of large quantities of yarn, but it is fine for surface applications such as painting. You paint cottons and silks which have been wetted out in a solution of water with fixative, let the yarn dry, then either steam it or put it in the clothes dryer for 30 minutes at high heat for fixing.

Procion MX is a powder with a complete color range. Stock solutions made with powder have a short life of a few days, and after the fixative is applied the dye lasts only four hours, so each time you use the dye you will probably need new stock solutions. Fixatives are washing soda for cellulose fibers and silk, and vinegar for wool and silk. The same methods for variegated dyeing on cellulose as Liquid Procion H will work, omitting the heat. If you use vinegar for silk or wool, heat is necessary.

Cibacron F has definite advantages over Procions. In the first place, the water in the bath may be calculated at 30 times the weight of fiber, which makes it easier to stir the bath for leveling, and less vigorous stirring mean less damage to silk and wool. For the same reason (more water) it is easier to level. In the second place, the stock solutions made from powder will stand (without fixative) for a month or even longer, so you do not need to make stock solutions for every dye run.** It comes in a full range of colors. For best results, however, the temperature of the dye bath must be higher than required for the Procions, which means a slightly different approach.

* Batching is the term used for applying the dye using washing soda as a fixative, wrapping the skeins airtight so that they stay wet, and allowing them to stand for 24 to 48 hours before finishing.

**Recent experiments show that Cibacron F stock solutions will retain their strength if they are placed in a freezer. The length of time they can be kept in this manner is a matter for further experiment.

Because I have done more experimentation with Cibacron F than the other fiber reactives, you will find in Appendix VII through X suggestions for level dyeing, variegated effects, fixatives and gradations.

Specific directions for dyeing with the fiber reactives and Inkodye are in the Appendix.

INKODYE

This is called a "vat dye" (whatever that means) and the texts mention it only in passing. I haven't found any directions for its use on yarn, so I have made up my own, based on the instructions for painting and batik on fabric. A description of the system appears in Appendix XI.

The liquid colors come in bottles and are activated by exposure to sunlight. Watching the colors appear is like looking at a Polaroid picture coming to life. It is safe for children if used outdoors and they enjoy seeing the colors appear like magic. The liquid dyes are simply diluted with water – direct from the bottle they are impossibly strong.

Finishing Textiles

With some exceptions, a textile is not finished when it comes from the loom. It must be washed, by methods varying from gentle hand washing to putting it through the washer and dryer. This is especially true of wools. If you are very smart you will allow enough warp to enable you to cut off a generous piece, cut it up into fairly large samples and put them through various finishing processes. Keep careful note of which method is used on which sample, and then select the one that produces the best cloth.

If you have never woven linen, you may be in for a surprise. Even if the yarn is beautiful on the spool, the fabric comes off the loom looking like gunnysack. It needs very harsh treatment, and the washing machine and hot water are ideal for this. However, never let the spin cycle go on for very long, because creases that are spun in may be there forever. Stop the spin frequently and turn the material. After the final rinse don't spin for more than a couple of minutes.

With wools, particularly singles, you may run into the phenomenon called "tracking," a diagonal crinkle which appears when it is fulled. It may turn up unexpectedly in any wool, but generally it happens only with a tightly twisted singles in a plain weave. I have had it occur in a yarn made of two plies of tightly spun singles. Sharon Alderman has several suggestions for dealing with the problem, of which the simplest is to steam press the textile hard before it is washed, and press it again while quite damp. (She doesn't mention the possibility that the fabric may revert to tracking in damp weather, but she lives in a dry section of the country.) Sometimes the best solution is just to learn to love the diagonal crepe effect.

Heavy fulling is the special area of Anita Mayer, author of books on handwoven clothing, and she has turned out some incredibly lovely examples. The method involves using a very open sett and weaving with the same number of picks per inch as the warp sett. This is tricky to beat evenly, but the fulling seems to erase differences in beat.

One of the most astonishing examples of what can happen with heavy fulling was woven by Betty Ladd, who set Harrisville singles at 10 epi and wove it in twill. After washing it in a machine for seven minutes in warm water, followed by cold rinses, the piece shrank 22% in length and 27% in width, and the result was incredibly light, thick and soft. Need we say that heavy fulling requires that the fabric must be woven much wider and longer than with regular fulling?

There are some fibers that are difficult-to-impossible to full – mohair, synthetics, and treated wools labeled "machine washable." If you combine these with wool and heavy fulling, you may get some strange results. Sample! Or have I said that before?

Some experienced weavers insist that you should only use a mild soap for washing handwovens. In this area what you get is a scum that it almost impossible to rinse out. Generally speaking, the best thing to use is a liquid detergent used for hand dishwashing – Ivory, Joy, Palmolive. (I have seen yarns labeled "Do Not Use Woolite". Bad news for Mr. Woolite.) Dyers use a liquid detergent called Synthrapol for removing loose dye, and it is great for finishing newly woven fabrics; a half-teaspoon makes a mountain of suds and you may spend a lot of time trying to rinse it out.

Dyers also use something called Orvus paste which, believe it or not, is to be found in your local shop for horse equipment. It is said to be the gentlest ever. Somehow I have never thought of horses as being that sensitive.

The best method of drying I have found is to roll the wet fabric over a textile core (from your fabric shop) padded with bath towels. After a few hours, remove the damp towels and put them through the dryer, reroll and let stand until dry. The fabric comes out nice and smooth, sometimes not even needing pressing. This is a good scheme for heavily fulled wools because often they come from the washing with ruffly edges and you can stretch the center areas while rolling. The whole process is rather demanding because if you roll in a crease you are in trouble. Anita Mayer finds this easiest to do on the floor, but she is young and lithe.

You may want to brush a wool fabric to blend the color, increase its warmth, and produce a soft surface. A nylon hair brush will work, but the best brush I have found is one intended to scrub pots or grills - it has rather long brass bristles, believe it or not. The brushing should be done in both warp and weft directions, not at an angle which may distort the weave, and is easiest to do while the fabric is damp, or while it is being steamed with an iron. If you are using variegated yarns, try brushing a sample; the colors are very much more subtle.

Handwoven silk is washed in much the same way as wool, but in warm water. In the next to last rinse, include a tablespoon of white vinegar to a gallon of water and allow to stand for a few minutes. Press with a steam iron over a padding of bath towels if you want to retain the handwoven look.

In the case of textured yarns, the bath towel on the ironing board is also a good idea. Very large lumps and bumps require a rather thick padding. Some boucles and slubs require no ironing at all.

Any of you who hate to iron place mats, or have members of the younger generation on your gift list (they won't iron anything, ever) might like this suggestion for mats and runners, gleaned from various sources and proved by experiment.

Forget linen, but mercerized cotton 10/3 or 5/2 makes nice place mats, and comes in good colors. Set at 18 epi and beaten square, they shrink about 15% each way. When they come off the loom, machine stitch and cut the pieces apart. Machine wash using hot water, but DO NOT SPIN which sets wrinkles that won't iron out. Take them from the machine dripping wet and smooth them out flat, stacking one on top of the other. Place a heavy weight on the top to squeeze out the water. When the excess has dripped out, stretch them on a very flat surface such as a formica counter or your washer, and allow to dry. No ironing is necessary.

Most of the above comes from an article by Clothilde Barrettt in an old Lily Mills "Practical Weaving Suggestions." Being timid by nature, I have modified the directions somewhat – she suggests putting the mats in the dryer after the excess water is squeezed out, after which they can be machine dried without ironing.

SLICK TRICKS

- **Cutting off samples:** This is included simply because over the years I have encountered weavers who were not taught this method in their beginning courses.

  The simplest and most effective cutoffs could be described as "stick-and-glue." Weave an inch or so of your warp in a yarn such as carpet warp. Insert a straight stick above this, and weave a new heading in carpet warp. Just below the dowel or stick run a line of glue, and let dry. Cut off your sample. To restore the tension, tie the stick in several places to the cloth beam rod. This restores the original tension. Each cut-off will use up about 5" of your warp, so allow this much extra when planning the length of the warp.

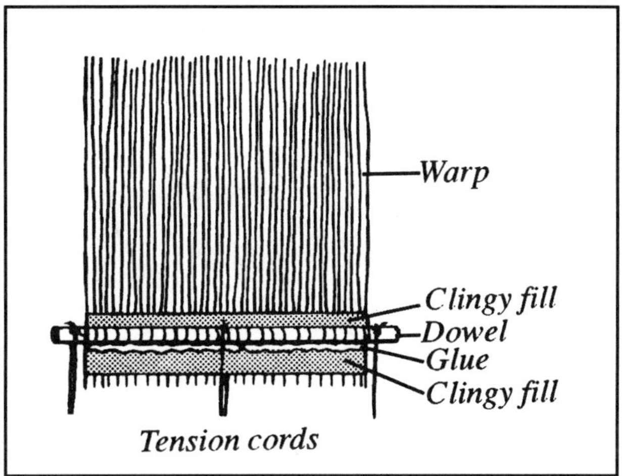

- One simple way of determining the amount of shrinkage on a sample is to lay the unwashed piece on a hard surface, tape it down and tape a length of shelf paper over it. Then with a soft pencil, or preferably a graphite stick from an art store, do a rubbing over the whole piece. When the sample is finished, lay it on the paper and the amount of shrinkage will be immediately apparent. This is especially useful if you have a raised pattern such as an overshot which needs to be matched.

- If you have a dry cleaner you can trust, a good steaming can make all the difference in the appearance of wools. There are also on the market pressing devices which give a truly professional finish, and which you can use at home. They are very expensive, and if I were ninety years younger I would invest in one.

Guilds, Study Groups and Conferences

"Sharing has brought us this far, and will take us farther still."
— Ralph Waldo Emerson

The more jaded among us sigh with resignation when gung-ho (as in "new") members of committees say brightly, "Let's send out a questionnaire." The response to questionnaires is apt to be so low as to make the results hardly worth the effort.

An exception to this rule was the questionnaire sent out to the applicants in the first go-around of the Certificate of Excellence program of the Handweavers Guild of America. We really needed to know, for future reference, where the applicants were coming from. The response was an unheard-of 80% of the questionnaires sent out. Of these, a very large number answered the question, "Where did you learn to weave?" with a succinct "Self-taught." It would probably have been more accurate, in most cases, if the replies had read, "Self-taught, with a lot of help from my friends."

A few handweavers, living mostly in remote places where they were not in touch with other weavers, have actually learned from books alone. The rest of us have taken lessons, however sketchy, and belong to guilds and study groups. We gradually acquire enough know-how from each other to get us to the state where we can help others.

People in the same field of work need each other, hence theater districts, art colonies, and the clustering of businesses in cities. However, the majority of handweavers are dedicated amateurs, and work mostly at home in scattered locations, about two to a square mile. Therefore it is natural for them to form associations with regular meetings, and to pool their resources and exchange ideas.

Mary Meigs Atwater started the use of the term "guild" by creating a national newsletter which she called the ShuttleCraft Guild. Local associations adopted the term, although "guild" historically has meant an organization more like a labor union or manufacturers' association than like a volunteer group for sharing information. Local guilds are still the backbone of handweaving education.

The committee in charge of a guild has a big assignment and much time-consuming work. The burn-out is correspondingly high. In fact when the Little Red Hen Awards are given out, the president, treasurer, membership chairman, program chairman, workshop chairman, and editor of the newsletter of any sizeable guild should be given gold medals, with diamonds on.

The program chairman particularly has a difficult job. How much of the program should be for beginners (which irritates the advanced craftsmen) and how much for the advanced weaver (which discourages the beginners)? And in which areas of interest? Where to hold meetings? Where to find speakers? And how do you finance it all? Weavers generally have a penchant for keeping dues as low as possible, and a proposal for raising them always provokes a bitter fight - this in a period when an ordinary movie will set you back $5 to $7 per person.

The workshop chairman has an equally difficult assignment, striking a balance between what their members can afford and meeting the high costs of the leaders' fees and their transportation. Again, the places to hold workshops are hard to find. In a doughnut city like Washington, if a workshop is held in an affordable and suitable place in Maryland, participants from Virginia may have to drive a solid hour in heavy traffic each way. And if held in Virginia the Maryland members suffer the same trauma. The District is the "hole in the doughnut" but has a great scarcity of suitable places.

If the local guild publishes a newsletter the editor has to be someone who has the patience of a saint in reminding committee members to submit announcements, preferably in plain English, by the publishing deadline, and then to get the material edited, printed and mailed.

A task that local guilds are well qualified to do is to put people with similar interests in touch with each other in order to form study groups. This is where you really get a lot of help from your friends. For best results they should be kept fairly small, but not so small that a flu epidemic or school holidays can wipe out a scheduled meeting.

Note the term "scheduled." Experience has shown that meetings should be on a set schedule, say the third Tuesday of each month, and agreement should be made that the date will not be changed. If members can say, "I can't do that, it's my study group day," they are more apt to arrange their lives to fit the schedule. Changes in dates can cause a great deal of telephoning by some burdened member.

A study group is a form of crisis intervention. It keeps you on an even keel, showing modified rapture when you turn up with what you think is wildly successful, and when you produce something you regard as a disaster they can comfort you and even make helpful suggestions to rescue you from despair. Very seldom do members copy each other's work. You think to yourself, "Great idea, but I'd do it this way or that," and wind up with, not a copy, but an entirely new approach.

The best study groups have a sort of informal program. A member may undertake to research an area and report to the group, or there may be a focus for the weaving year on some definite area, such as color, fashion, a certain weave, tapestry, knitting, warp setts, or fibers.

For weavers beginning to take an interest in dyeing, a study group whose members share the samples they make with the other members of the group, can shortcut the laborious process of accumulating samples.

On a larger scale, there are regional organizations of guilds, such as the Michigan League, the Midwest Conference, the New England Weavers Seminar, and big gatherings in the mountain states and on the West Coast. If you have never attended one of these, start saving your pennies and go. You will be introduced to new ideas or variations on old ones, both from the formal program and from the midnight gatherings in dorm or hotel rooms. There is an exhilaration about a weavers' conference that comes about in no other way. Never mind if you don't know anybody - you soon will.

A last request from my husband before I leave for a conference has always been, "Try to get some sleep."

Then there's the Big One – the biennial Convergence of the Handweavers Guild of America. Here you will meet the international stars of handweaving. A big weavers' conference is like a visit from your grandchildren – you're thrilled when it starts and secretly relieved when it's over.

Lest you think that all this is done with mirrors, please think again – it's all done with the blood, sweat, toil and tears of volunteers. Each of the members of the committee that organized the first Convergence at Detroit spent most of their time for two years to get that first gathering on its feet. We weren't helped by an uneasy fear that the whole thing might flop, and we were committing the newly-formed HGA to a large expenditure and betting that it would succeed.

The original format was set in Mary Sayler's kitchen, a meeting which lasted most of one night. This is not to overlook the hard work of the Michigan guilds, who used every pair of handweaving hands in the region.

In some respects, things haven't turned out the way we originally visualized them. We thought, for example, that the "seminars" would consist of small gatherings with an appointed leader who would lead a general discussion on the topic under consideration. In fact, they have developed into one-session workshops. The leaders come armed with slides and set speeches, and there is far too little chance to ask questions and exchange information.

Slides are really necessary for very large gatherings, and are perhaps better than unillustrated speeches, but they have become a crutch. If you attend many seminars at a conference you may come away from a day's attendance with burning eyes and a sense of frustration. Sometimes slides are used when they are completely inappropriate. I once watched a seminar leader try to teach eight-harness double weave to about 200 people, using slides. The only people who understood were the ones who knew how to do eight-harness double weave to start with.

Longer workshops are not always free of these types of flaws. I was in a three-day workshop in which the teacher brought so many slides of her work and talked so constantly (admittedly with great enthusiasm) that her students never had a chance to use any of the large number of art materials they had assembled in advance.

Who was it who said, "The greatest enemy of learning is the talking teacher?" And: "Out of 100 people, one will make things happen, nine will watch things happen, and 90 will look up and say, "what happened?"

We have a family saying, "When all else fails, read the directions," A sentence from a printed instruction booklet that came with a new clothes dryer said, "See pages 3 and 4 for exhausting details." Right! Well put. But if you leave your notes unused for too long after a workshop is over, you may find the directions mean nothing.

Housekeeping and the Handweaver

The trouble with housekeeping is that it's so daily.
—Neolithic Housewife, circa 4004 B.C.

I was once asked by a smart-alecky teenager (a male chauvinist pig in training) why it is that all the great chefs, artists and musicians have been men. My retort, "Because they had wives," quite clearly puzzled him, because what does a housewife do besides cook and watch the soap operas?

Maybe you are haunted by an upbringing like mine. Your mother was a meticulous housekeeper who believed sincerely that cleanliness is next to godliness. All female children were brain-washed to believe that the following were required of them for the rest of their lives: clutter picked up; kitchen cleaned and in order (dishes washed and in the cupboard right after a meal); out of season clothing protected against dirt and moths; bathroom scrubbed; clean and mended underwear worn at all times in case you were in an accident.

For some reason this early training has never been applied to males, which explains why most of them know exactly where to find things, but can't remember where the same objects belong when it's time to put them away. If you think all this has changed with the advent of feminism, you are deluded. A lady who practices law in partnership with her husband has complained that he often will ask, "Honey, where are my clean socks?"

Weavers have to be naturally good organizers or they couldn't design and produce anything. Hence those with even rudimentary consciences worry about not being able to organize their housekeeping chores and keep on weaving.

Years ago someone gave me a still-cherished card depicting Charlie Brown's friend, Pigpen, surrounded as always by clouds of dirt, with the following comment, "Neatness is man's greatest fallacy." It is posted in my workroom and despite my early upbringing I try to believe the sentiments.

Over the years, observations show that there are three kinds of weavers :

(1) The free soul: she simply doesn't care whether the house is in order or not, and doesn't mind being called a layabout by non-weaving acquaintances. She has lots of time to weave.

(2) The ideal housewife: she is highly thought of by friends and family because the household is always in order. Her bookcases can pass a white-glove inspection, and she is not undone by the certainty that the mess she has just cleaned up will reappear tomorrow. She can find anything on request without prior notice. She is an expert in crisis management so can cope with problems as they come up – holiday meals, sick children, house guests, breakdowns of equipment. She answers all letters promptly. She spends specified times on daily chores, plus blocks of time on general work such as dusting lampshades and discarding old magazines. Her checkbook always balances. She never stops to frighten herself by estimating the number of individual objects in the house that need dusting, sorting, washing, pressing, mending and being put back in place. She makes frequent checks on the health and happiness of her friends. She has a Black Belt in shopping. She is indeed a paragon. The only problem is that she never has time to weave.

(3) The rest of us: We would like to be like either Mrs. (1) or Mrs. (2) but can't seem to choose which, so keep telling ourselves to care a little less or organize a little better.

I wonder whether Dr. Freud, who practiced psychiatry on middle-class women in the heyday of domestic servants, ever investigated anyone trying without help to combine household management with a career. Or for that matter, whether he ever psychoanalyzed a domestic servant.

In case you think I'm complaining because I'm a bad organizer, wrong again. At the age of twenty I took charge of housing 1200 high school athletes for a track meet in a small town. (Lost nobody, and nobody slept on gratings.) A lot of years later I was one of a group who organized a Guild weaving school which, I am proud to say, is still being run largely on the basis we established. I was on the committee that organized the first, and extremely scary, HGA Convergence; my particular responsibility was the workshops at Cranbrook. (Some real bloopers still haunt my nightmares.) I was one of four who set up the HGA Certificate of Excellence program and edited the handbook still in use.

For serendipity, and it shouldn't be a total loss, these activities gave me a lot of treasured friends, and a lot of enemies.

All this is recounted to show that I admit I am a good organizer when there is a well-defined objective. It must also be admitted that during these undertakings my life was a welter of bad housekeeping, neglect of friends and family who deserved better, frantic last-minute holiday shopping, and other faults of poor organization.

A truly compulsive organizer can spend more time figuring out the most efficient way of doing some chore than it would take to pitch in willy-nilly and do it.

This all came to mind recently when I was in the kitchen talking on the phone to Virginia Brooks, a friend. Suddenly I looked around and exclaimed, "My kitchen floor is grungy." Her reply was, "Well, take off your glasses."

If you were expecting any words of wisdom from me about how to combine housekeeping with weaving, I'm sorry. It all boils down to "Take off your glasses."

Every now and then my frustrations over the housekeeping/weaving dichotomy bursts out into doggerel, as follows:

Poetic Outburst In Football Season

(with apologies to the shade of Ogden Nash)

In far Peru there lives a weaver
Who never heard of Redskin Fever.
She sits and spins and weaves and dyes
And never tries to win First Prize.
No doors to lock, because no doors,
No muddy tracks on new-scrubbed floors.
No bills to pay in large amounts
(No credit cards, no charge accounts).
No shrubs to plant, complete with rootball,
No PTA, no Sunday football. . . .
If you will watch the wide receiver
I think I'll go and join that weaver.

Murphy's Law for Handweavers

The original Murphy's Law reads: "If anything can go wrong, it will." I don't know who Mr. Murphy was, but his law applies to weaving as much as it does to any other activity. Below are some of the areas where things can go wrong, with corollaries.

I. Setting up the Warp

(a) An error in threading will not become evident until the weaving is well started.

(b) Such an error will occur where it is the maximum amount of trouble to correct: e.g., in the center of the warp, plus or minus 2%.

(c) In correcting the problem, two or more unrelated errors will appear.

(d) It will take longer to correct these errors than it took to thread the warp in the first place.

II. The Loom

(a) If a part loosens and falls into the interior of the loom, the fact will not become evident until the piece develops peculiar errata; e.g., somewhere about the midpoint of the textile.

(b) The missing piece will land in the most inaccessible place, requiring maximum gymnastics to fish it out.

(c) Restoring the part to its place will require disassembly of the loom.

III. Materials

(a) Although your yarn storage space may be full to bursting, when you design a new project you will find that you don't have quite enough yarn to complete it, and must order more.

(b) Due to differences in dye lots, you will be unable to combine the new yarn with the stock on hand which, with the inevitable leftovers of both batches, compounds storage problems.

(c) Your long-suffering family will call you a yarn hoarder.

IV. Guilding

(a) If you speak up in a meeting to make a suggestion you have just volunteered to implement it.

(b) The more capable you are at doing a job and the harder you work, the more golden opportunities will be offered you to take on more taxing chores.

(c) If you decide that you must stay home from workshops and put into practice what you've learned in previous ones, the first workshop you skip will be a once-only wonder and you'll regret for the rest of your life that you missed it.

V. Teaching

(a) In any class you undertake to teach, at least one student will know more than you do and prove it by asking leading questions.

(b) After every workshop you prepare you will discover things that you should have included, but didn't. As a result, preparations for every class will have to start from square one.

(c) When all examples are collected for travel, you will look like a gypsy caravan, and at least one important item will be left behind.

VI. Dyeing

(a) If you are a natural dyer, you are destroying the environment; if you are a chemical dyer, you are polluting it.

(b) You can stand forever over a pot of dye waiting for it to simmer, but if you answer the phone or leave the room for an instant, the pot will immediately come to a full rolling boil.

(c) Ikat:

(1) If you are trying for a definite pattern, the yarn will slip in the weaving and blur into no-pattern.

(2) If you are trying for unpatterned colors, your warp and/or weft will form an insistent repeat.

(3) If you are dyeing a plain color, the skein ties will be a bit too tight and will create a pattern (involuntary ikat). If you are dyeing ikat, the ties will be a bit loose and the dye will leak under them (involuntary un-ikat).

(d) Color:

(1) You may look at a pot of dye and decide the color is not quite right. There are then two possibilities: add a little more dye and regret it; or don't add a little more dye and regret it.

(2) If you dye in daylight, your colors will look terrible in artificial light; e.g., red-violet becomes brown, blue-violet becomes navy. If you dye in artificial light, your colors will look terrible in daylight.

(3) If you are trying for uneven color, the result will be completely level (one too many stirs); if you are trying for level color the result will be mottled (one too few stirs).

(e) Dyes that will not work on some fibers will stain them in accidents (red-sock-in-white-wash principle). The stains will not be removable by any known bleach.

VII. Design

(a) If you try for the simple and elegant, the result will be deadly dull.

(b) If you try for the striking and bold, the result will be garish.

VIII. Writing

(a) If you are typing hand-outs, errors, such as typos and misplaced clauses, will not appear in your original manuscript.

(b) The minute the material appears in print the errors will glare at you.

IX. Housewifery

(a) Any effort to establish a regular schedule allowing you time to weave will collapse not later than the second week of application.

(b) If household appliances are to break down, it will occur on Friday evening.

(c) If your work space gets too cluttered to cope with and you decide to throw away some notes, books, samples and yarn ends, you will need them the day after the trash pickup.

(d) Dinner has to be cooked when you're tired and hungry.

The Peripatetic Handweaver

Who was it who said, "Life is what happens to you when you're making other plans"? The most unplanned thing about my life was marrying a lawyer who became involved with air transport. Since the last thing an air executive wants to do in his spare time, if any, is to take a holiday involving long airplane rides, it is the clear duty of his wife to do the family traveling on those free tickets. So whenever a weaver proposed a jaunt to a handweaving area, I was right there with freebie in hand. This accounts for my great good luck in seeing many of the so-called "primitive" weaving areas. Besides, it became widely known during the early days of the HGA that I could attend meetings without the organization's having to pay for transportation, so I was assigned to various interesting committees and met a lot of interesting weavers.

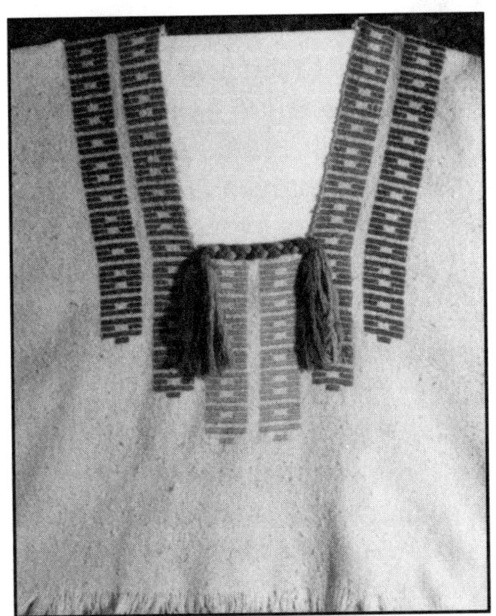

Sometimes, trips planned without particular reference to weaving turned up with surprises, and sometimes places where you might expect to find handweaving produced none that you could find – Italy, for instance.

If you are thinking in terms of a trip where handweaving is to be seen, perhaps the following patchy notes might help you to decide.

For the weaver, Mexico City has a huge and fascinating archaeological museum. It has rooms and rooms of handwoven clothing, classified as to area and period. My husband, the most patient of men, spent two whole days with me looking at everything from the monstrous statue at the entrance (the Aztecs were masters of the gruesome in art) to the very last backstrap loom. I'm sorry to say, though, that the smog in Mexico City is said to be the worst in the world.

If you want to see contemporary handweaving walking around on people, Oaxaca in Mexico is one place to go. The markets are full of handweaving for sale.

Nearby are the ruins of a religious center called Mitla, and here is where unforewarned weavers are apt to have palpitations at the sight of many low, long stone buildings inlaid in mosaic with carefully cut triangles, rectangles, Greek keys, and parallelograms, forming patterns obviously taken from weaving and expanded to a great scale. Walls are in the form of panels surrounded by plain stone frames and each panel is in a different overall design. Since most ancient buildings in Mexico were painted, it is probable that the patterns were decorated in colors like the woven pieces they imitated. The buildings were ancient and nearly forgotten long before the arrival of the Spanish.

Your Mitla guide will tell you that the local weavers copy the designs from the building, although they are all clearly weaving-derived. If the designs were not weaving-derived, then Mitla must have been visited in ancient times by weavers from Europe, the Middle East, Africa and Asia, who promptly went home and copied them.

Yucatan is a part of Mexico, but artistically in the orbit of the Maya. The facades of the buildings at Uxmal show a similar approach to decoration as do those of Mitla, although the derivation from weaving is less obvious. For instance, a stylized snake in stone mosaic may run clear across the facade of a long building, but it is made up of squares and triangles. The connection with weaving design is still evident. The Yucatecans apparently lost their weaving heritage, probably because the Spanish put the populace to work raising sisal for cordage. In any case, you will find very little handweaving to buy or to admire.

Farther to the south, in Guatemala, handweaving is still a major occupation and the skill displayed by weavers working on backstrap looms is nothing short of astonishing. (It is fair to say that the simpler the equipment the more freedom of design, and the more skill required.) The people in the villages are obviously very poor, but their costumes rejoice in brilliant colors and intricate designs. To a great extent each village has its own particular patterns by which the knowledgeable can tell which area the weaver comes from. You will be so overcome with the skill of these backstrap weavers that you may begin to feel inferior, but remember that these little people might be equally impressed with some of your skills, such as wheeling a two-ton car through heavy traffic. If you go there, carry your rabbit's foot against the possibility of earthquake and war, and take lots of money to spend in the markets.

In the recent past, somebody tipped off the weavers of Guatemala that their used materials - much-worn but handsome and fast colors – would make attractive shirts to sell to tourists, so they cut up their old ikat skirts, for which they are famous, and turned them into shirts. A later canny calculation was that anything purple sells like mad, so many shirts were overdyed this color, with spectacular results when the purple blends with the original colors. The group that toured Guatemala after the canceled Florida Convergence were completely carried away. They searched out these brilliant shirts, wore them on the last night of the tour, and turned purple. It seems that the shirts were just dipped in purple dye and dried without rinsing.

Peru is another country that is famous for its weaving, especially on the high central plateau. Again, it is done entirely with backstrap looms and for a very good reason – where the weaving populace lives, there are absolutely no trees. If you wanted a floor loom you would have to import it. There is also no wood for shipping crates or cartons, so produce on the railway from Lake Titicaca to Cuzco is packed in woven bags. You see them stacked on the station platforms, and they are very obviously handwoven because here and there the bags have woven motifs in brilliant colors. Why not? If you must weave bags for shipping containers you might as well have some fun doing it.

There are many small backstreet shops in Lima which sell scraps of handwoven cloth, and nobody has a clue about where they come from or how old they are. Pots, not textiles, are used by archaeologists for dating buried treasure.

Peru has a corner on some of the most marvelous handwovens in the world: the mummy bundles of the Nazca area south of Lima. The trove is in the big public museum in Lima and displayed on life-sized figures dressed as they must have been dressed in life. Sad to report, they are deteriorating. I saw them five years apart and the first time they were gorgeous; the second time they were a mass of fuzz from decaying threads. What they are like now, I don't even want to think about. Lima is a very damp place (though it never rains, it is always cloudy) and the handwovens preserved in the desert for hundreds of years are slowly becoming just lumps of fiber. The worst of it is that the Lima Museum is said to have dozens of the bundles still not unwrapped, and stored somewhere. You can only hope that they are stored in air-conditioned vaults, but it's doubtful.

If you want to see these masterpieces in something like their original appearance, go to a big museum such as the Philadelphia or the Natural History in New York, where they are displayed in glass cases, hermetically sealed.

There is an ancient and massive religious center, Pachacamac, near Lima, It is a mountain of crumbling rubble surrounded by its own dust. In the 1970's, when I was there last, you could pick up fragments of weaving out of the dirt. And nobody cared but us handweavers.

The definitive work for handweavers on Peruvian textiles is contained in two monographs by Harriet Tidball, *Peru: Textiles Unlimited.* Part I concerns itself mostly with history, and Part II goes into the structure of the fabrics.

Greece is a place you visit to see the classical ruins, although there are many handwovens to be found. But weaving was not on my mind when we stopped overnight in a town called Nauplia (or Nauplion) to visit the ruins of Tiryns, a palace with romantic associations with the Trojan War. The building, as it stands, is a cluster of huge gray weathered stones, and you have to take the word of the guidebook that there were fountains and treasuries and gaily painted rooms.

Tiryns is off the tourist track and we had to take a taxi with a very cross driver who kept honking the horn for us to hurry. It was while exploring the foundations that we came across a recently excavated chamber, long and narrow with rough walls and a curved ceiling. The ceiling stones were lumpy but rounded and polished very shiny. We might have been wondering yet about that phenomenon, except that a young archaeologist, also exploring on his own, appeared and explained that after the building was abandoned, local shepherds had used it to shelter their sheep. The floor, over the centuries, gradually filled with rubble until at last it had been raised until the sheep's coats rubbed against the ceiling. It's mind-boggling to think how many years it would take to wear rough masonry smooth just by rubbing it with living wool.

Italy has relatively little for the handweaver to study, but recently I did a double-take at a picture of the Doge's palace in Venice. When you are looking at the building, your eye is always taken by admiration of the lower part with its arches, quatrefoil windows and elaborate Gothic capitals. Until you study a photograph, you don't notice that the sheer wall above all this frippery is inlaid in squares of marble in three colors in a pattern that can only be described as 14-end point twill woven as drawn in, complete with the little cross in the center of each diamond. This can be woven on a four-harness loom, but perhaps it would be best not to try it in marble.

Roofs in the country around Beaune in France have similar patterns in colored tile, particularly variations on Rose Path.

In Paris, I dragged my tolerant husband to the Cluny to see the famous "Lady and the Unicorn" tapestries. He was conditioned by a bad experience in Spain, where they are inordinately proud of their Baroque tapestries with elaborate borders, detailed depiction of the exploits of forgotten heroes, and dust. When we came to the huge circular room in the Cluny where the "Unicorn" is hung, he came to a dead stop and was nearly speechless. Finally, he managed, "I thought all tapestries were ugly."

The Unicorn tapestries must be the most beautiful ever made. By a nice coincidence, we were in Paris when the chestnuts were in bloom and the tapestries show them very clearly though (by tapestry convention) they are somewhat out of proportion to the human and animal figures.

If you are touring the Loire Valley looking at chateaux, you should be aware that about a half-day's drive from Tours there is a spectacular tapestry museum in a castle at Angers. In a building especially designed for it, there is a dimly lighted room where the "Apocalypse" tapestries are shown. They are about a century older than the Unicorns, and believe it or not, there are seven of them, each eighty feet long and twenty feet high. Since there is really a limit to the amount of time a weaver can spend indulging her mania when traveling with non-weavers, that was all I saw at the museum, but it was enough to boggle the mind for years. The Unicorn tapestries are romantically beautiful, but from a design standpoint the Apocalypse tapestries are far more impressive, and not just because of their enormous size.

In England, the Victoria and Albert Museum in London has the famous Raphael cartoons for the tapestries now in the Vatican. They are worth seeking out because they are said to represent the first time a painter made full-size cartoons to be copied in tapestry and, from the weaver's point of view, the first step on the downward path to the baroque tapestries. After Raphael, painters took over and weavers were expected to copy them literally. Yarn colors went from about 30 (at the time of the Unicorn tapestries) to, so they say, about 30,000. Tapestry weaving degenerated to the point where weaving was the work of artisans, not artists.

The "V & A" has hundreds of tapestries to be seen, many of them the beautiful Gothic tapestries woven before or shortly after 1500 AD. While you are there, you might want to look at them.

England also has the famous "Christ in Glory," apparently the largest tapestry ever woven (78 x 35 feet) which is given pride of first place in the new, modern and lovely Coventry cathedral. Go see the cathedral, never mind the tapestry. A famous English weaver, who shall be nameless, calls it "the largest piece of seersucker in the world." Unlike most tapestries, this one is hung with the warp in vertical position, and apparently the weavers (French) didn't trust the strength of the linen warp, so every ten inches or so there is a nylon cord to help support the enormous weight. The sad result is that the linen warp ends stretch and shrink with the variations of humidity in the air and the nylon cord doesn't, so "seersucker" is a good description. The design was by the painter Sutherland. Sorry to say in the enlargement to 78 x 35 feet, something was lost. The figure of Christ will remind you of a large bumblebee on a vast green ground.

Washington, D.C.'s museums have their share of beautiful tapestries, but one specially woven for its site is not one of them – it hangs in the gorgeous modern addition to the National Gallery of Art known as the East Building, and it looks as if it had been designed with a chain saw. PBS has a film showing the weaving and hanging of this huge affair, which apparently weighs tons and is so heavy it had to be installed with the aid of cranes. Tapestry lovers, unless they are consumed with curiosity, should avert their eyes.

Japan is a weaver's and designer's heaven. It seems to be the only industrialized nation that really appreciates the special qualities of handwoven fabrics. I was lucky enough to go there with Hallye Spurkel of Honolulu, who lived most of her life in Hawaii and collected Japanese textiles. She came armed with a list of what to see and where to shop, and even arranged for a Japanese handweaver and her English-speaking sister to take us to a silk-weaving village north of Tokyo.

For the enlightenment of dyers, ikat warps are stretched outdoors in long wooden troughs with slots in the sides to guide the tying of the resist knots which form the pattern. To offset the motifs in weaving, half of the warp was then run over a wooden frame, triangular in section, which shortened it a few inches so the pattern appeared in two alternate positions when the fabric was woven. All this is of course economically possible only where the patterns are traditional so the trough can be used over and over.

One establishment was dyeing with indigo in a large round area filled with huge plastic barrels with nice firm lids. I stood on one while the dyeing was going on, but hastily retreated when I realized what the vats contained – very unpleasant to fall into.

Japanese who can speak English love to talk to you, and the first thing they ask is, "Where do you live?" "New York" was greeted with "Ohs," "Honolulu" with "Ahs," but "Minneapolis" left them blank. Long afterwards I realized I should have said "Minnetonka" and brought down the house. It seems that one of the first pieces in English studied by Japanese children begins "By the shores of Gitchegoomee, by the shining big sea waters ......"

Leaves From A Weaver's Memory Book

One of the pleasures of attending weavers' conferences is sitting up all night in dorm or hotel rooms and talking about weaving – and weavers.

You may think of weavers as mostly housewives, but the truth is that they come from many professions, not to mention two sexes. They are the source of many tales.

When I was at the University of Montana, there was a professor of mathematics who was a campus legend because of his far-out hobby – something called handweaving, whatever that meant. His name was Dr. William Bateman, and is known principally to multiple-harness weavers of an experimental turn of mind.

There is a lawyer in the Midwest who has occasion to fly to Washington frequently in the company plane. As part of her luggage she carries an inkle loom.

An avid camper who attended the Fort Collins Convergence stayed with her family at a nearby campground. Being a student of folkways, she decided to launder the sock accumulation in a nearby creek, by pounding them with rocks. The results were suitably clean, but full of holes. The rest of the trip she planned to patronize the local laundromats.

A tapestry weaver in Chicago is an expert belly-dancer.

The Best-in-Show award at the Michigan League one year went to Eunice Anders of Canada, who produced a beautiful and intricate three-dimensional hanging on eight harnesses. It had to be registered with Canadian customs on leaving Canada to avoid payment of duty on the return trip. The officer looked it over and issued a certificate reading "Wall hanging, home-made."

An anecdote in "Interweave" Magazine (now "Handwoven") is so funny it bears repeating. Fred Gerber, a weaver and dyer in Florida, was offering some beautiful hand-dyed scarves for sale. A woman was filled with admiration but jibbed at the price, so Mr. Gerber explained the long processes that went into them. The customer was unimpressed, remarking, "Oh, but you had so much fun!" Moral: if you want a fair price for your work, don't enjoy it.

Mary Meigs Atwater, whether young weavers have ever heard of her or not, is the patron saint of modern American handweaving. For some reason, she began researching it when it was dead as a craft, except in the Southern Highlands where it survived mostly because many of the people were so poor they had to find some way of providing clothing and household articles for themselves. This is not to say that what they wove was ugly; it was simply disregarded by the world in general. In various areas, such as Pennsylvania, New England and the South, there were collections of handweaving and drafts, and Mrs. Atwater made it her business to visit all she could reach.

Her husband was a mining engineer and the Atwaters lived in Butte, Montana during its wildest years as a coppermining boom town. There is a legend that she always carried a loaded revolver in her handbag in the days when the National Rifle Association was but a pup. When you consider what Butte was like when she lived there, it's no wonder she went armed, if she really did.

There are many tales about Mrs. Atwater, and there are still some of her former students around, but never have I heard anyone refer to her by her first name. She was "Mrs. Atwater" to all. She was very proud of her maiden name and justly so, since her father was General Montgomery Meigs of the Union Army in the Civil War. His monument is the stately building in Washington, D.C. now known as the National Building Museum, which he built as headquarters for the postwar Pension Fund. It's worth looking at when you're in Washington, D.C. because of the handsome interior and because on the outside it has a terra-cotta frieze of horsemen, artillery and soldiers.

Mrs. Atwater's work is amazing in its scope and full of basic information about oddball techniques, very precisely described. Her drafts are classics of art on their own, and her ShuttleCraft Guild Bulletin was largely responsible for the revival of handweaving.

On the word of my mother, I can claim acquaintance with Mrs. Atwater because she used to come to our house when I was a child. I'm sorry to say I don't remember.

Her most famous pupil was probably the late Harriet Tidball, who was her assistant in publishing the "Bulletin" and who continued the ShuttleCraft Guild after her mentor retired. Under Mrs. Tidball the publication later flowered into the famous monographs, which are still in print.

Harriet was a brilliant technician, and it is a pity that her career was cut short by her early death. Her friends agree that she had much more to offer the world of handweaving and was really just hitting her stride when we lost her. The great concept of her monographs was that any draft or weave had many more possible interpretations than the classical forms. Her study of the double weave launched a whole world of new ideas, and her monograph on surface interest textiles started a new trend in the design of handwovens. She was not really a great designer herself, but she always encouraged the development of new concepts, and published them.

She was generous to a fault and you had to be a bit careful about admiring anything she owned – she was quite ready to present it to you. The other side of this generosity was that she assumed other people were equally generous, and she got into occasional trouble by being unconscious of the fact that before publishing ideas she should really ask permission of the originator.

She wrote many pieces that were published in the "ShuttleCraft Guild Bulletin" during the time of Mrs. Atwater. They were not usually signed, but it is easy to detect her work because of a repertoire of words she consistently misspelled – "consistantly" and "treadeling" for example. She used to laugh about one long-term subscriber to the publication who, when she received a new issue, sat down and wrote, carefully pointing out the errors in spelling. Harriet always wrote a polite acknowledgment, but misspelled the same words in the next issue. Some of these characteristic misspellings appear in the monographs still in print.

She did a lot of traveling to centers of handweaving around the world - the Far and Near East, Mexico, Peru, Guatemala and North Africa. She had great technical knowledge and an eye for good design. Everywhere she went, she brought back examples – some very ancient – of beautiful handweaving on which she based some of her writing.

In the last months of her life she was in the process of writing her will. After much research, she decided to leave her collection to the University of Washington and to endow the University with enough funds to classify and preserve it, and make it accessible to students. She stopped by Minneapolis on her way from Seattle to consult my husband about the terms of her will, which she was writing and rewriting so that it would conform to her wishes. He advised her to sign the most recent draft, which she could always revise later. She died intestate very suddenly a few weeks later. According to the laws of Michigan her estate went to her next of kin. Since some of them were minors, there was no way of providing the endowment she planned. Fortunately her brother carried out her wishes and gave the collection to the University. At the Seattle Convergence there was a panicky rumor circulating among the handweavers present that since the University of Washington lacked the funds to care for the collection, it would be turned over to the Drama Department for use as costumes. Fortunately, this turned out not to be true, and the pieces are available for study.

Grace Blum was a fascinating and humorous lady who lived in the Chicago area and was a specialist in weaving with fine yarns. She sold yarn by mail and was one of principal sources of the Bernat wool known as Fabri, a soft 2/18's worsted which was very popular with weavers in the Fifties. When Bernat dropped it from their list, she had a large stock on hand and kept weavers supplied for a long time. In 1960 she published, and marketed, a remarkable book entitled *Functional Overshot,* which has 33 actual samples. She took as a starting point a traditional small pattern and threaded her loom with 20/2 buff cotton at 30 epi. All the swatches were woven on this set-up with different yarns and treadlings, producing really surprising variations which it is hard to believe came from the same threading. At the time the price of $16.50 was considered to be out of sight and it took her a long time to sell all the copies. It is a priceless source of ideas, and now that it is out of print, a copy is worth a small fortune.

Grace was the source of the following hilarious tale told in weavers' gatherings. She had an acquaintance who was an executive in a firm manufacturing woolen textiles. He complained that the company had some fine warp yarns left from a discontinued line and was looking for a buyer. After ascertaining that the yarn was on spools she offered to buy it for resale to handweavers.

In due time a truck backed into her driveway and unloaded huge drums of yarn, so many that they filled her garage. So far, so good, but on inspection she found that the drums were wound with ends of warp at about 60 per inch – in effect warp beams ready to thread. The last I heard she was still seeking suggestions from her many weaving friends on how to unwind simultaneously (from the very heavy drums) 3600 ends of very fine yarn.

The first Convergence workshops at Cranbrook had one never-to-be- forgotten episode. One of the workshop leaders was English, new to this country, and her group was scheduled to create a knotted "environment" in an outdoor setting. The leader started a day early with two volunteer assistants, who must have been city- dwelling types, because when we arrived on the scene we found that the place they had chosen out of all the magnificent Cranbrook grounds was knee-deep in poison ivy, so thick that we didn't even walk over to warn the workers, just stood and shouted. Luckily the three involved were not allergic to poison ivy, but we had a bad fright. The project was moved indoors.

Barbara Wittenberg was hospitality chairman of the workshops, and organized a lavish party for the technical staff and the committees, concluding with a large cake labeled, **WELCOME FELLOW LOOMATICS."**

Peter Collingwood's *Techniques of Rug Weaving* is worth owning even if you are not a rug weaver, because it is full of practical information on many of the problems encountered by weavers in any area of the craft. He has a genius for making things clear by sketches and explication. His book of tablet weaving is equally helpful, and the one on sprang is said to be equally clear, but I don't own a copy because my one attempt at sprang ended in disaster and I never did understand any of it above the cat's-cradle.

Mr. Collingwood is equally talented as a parodist. He taught sprang to a group who studied various phases of weaving in Canterbury in 1973, and at a reunion of the students at the San Francisco Convergence he read a parody on Dante's Inferno depicting the tortures of people learning sprang, with the maximum agony reserved for the teachers of sprang, who were confined to the lowest depths of Hell.

His masterpiece in this area is printed in ShuttleCraft Monograph #8, *Peter Collingwood, His Weaves and Weaving.* It is a send-up of the fundamentalists among weavers, depicting the career of Elsie Cutch and her friends (George Weld, Marjorie Fustic, Sir Indigo-Jones). You should really read it, but the gist is that Elsie was such a fundamentalist that she not only built her own loom but spun the yarn to make the heddles and the apron, from cotton she raised in Africa and linen she retted with water from Belgium.

Some years after this was published, I told the author how much I enjoyed reading it. He admitted that it was intended to be one of a series, but he gave up the idea because of objections from the traditionalists, of whom England has a plentiful supply. His next episode was to be entitled **Colonel Raddle.** It's our loss.

This comes to mind because of the following paragraph from the June 1988 issue of Spin-Off which refers to directions for varicolored dyeing:

> "Even if you don't spin or haven't the time, you can enjoy the results of this technique. The following project calls for commercial yarn, although, of course, your own handspun can be used. Do not feel guilty about using commercial yarn. Dyeing is as much a craft as spinning and should not be dependent on it".

I find this disclaimer rather astonishing. Does anyone think that painters should go back to grinding their own mineral colors, or should they take the gifts that chemistry has given them and get on with their art? Or should they feel obliged to go out and catch some badgers or sables (or whatever) and make their own brushes?

Because handweaving started as a revival of cottage production methods, there has always been a tendency to think that any shortcuts should be ruled out. Some of us are unreconstructed rebels against that point of view.

You probably have been at a loss as to how to describe yourself in relationship to weaving. "Hobbyist" equate you with people who collect matchbook covers, and "Professional" overstates the case for many of us. The unabridged Merriam-Webster gives the word the following definition: "...2. Characteristic of or conforming to the standards of a profession, as, distinctly <u>professional</u> work. 3. Engaging for livelihood or gain in an activity pursued, usually or often, for non-commercial satisfaction by amateurs..."

That lets some of us in, and are we surprised! But there ought to be some way of removing the stigma from the word "amateur." Originally it meant someone who pursued an occupation from love of it, but nowadays it is usually taken to mean "dabbler" or "tyro." After all, the people who did the basic research in natural history, electricity and chemistry were proud to consider themselves amateurs. Among Americans, Jefferson was an amateur in archaeology and architecture, and Franklin in electricity. Amateurs of the world, arise!

Sometimes weavers are taken aback to find out how little people in general understand about what you do. For example, I was asked by the program director of a garden club, doubtless desperate for a speaker, to come to a meeting and talk about handweaving. Pride compelled me to work very hard on a speech which would minimize puzzling technical details, and I brought my latest triumph to show. I spent quite a few moments trying to describe how it was designed and woven. During the question period, I was asked, "What other colors does it come in?"

The following dialogue was overheard between two painters working on the interior of my studio:

YOUNG ASSISTANT: What does she do with these big machines?

BOSS PAINTER: She does weaving. It takes a lifetime to learn and the method was lost for hundreds of years.

Every now and then I have been asked by someone whether I know any prayers appropriate to weavers. The following was read during a memorial service for Harriet Tidball.

Not until the loom is silent
And the shuttles cease to fly
Will God unfold the fabric
And explain the reason why
The dark threads are as needful
In the weaver's skillful hand
As the threads of gold and silver
In the pattern He has planned.

(Author: Father Tabb)

Bibliography

Albers, Josef
Interaction of Color. Yale University Press, New Haven, Connecticut, 1963

Alderman, Sharon and Wertenberger, Kathryn
Handwoven, Tailormade. Interweave Press, Loveland: Colorado, 1982

Baizerman, Suzanne and Searle, Karen
Finishes in the Ethnic Tradition. Dos Tejedoras, St. Paul, Minnesota, 1978

Blumenthal, Betsy and Kreider, Kathryn
Hands on Dyeing. Interweave Press, Loveland: Colorado, 1988

Bress, Helene
The Weaving Book: Patterns and Ideas. Scribners, New York 1981

Collingwood, Peter
Peter Collingwood: His Weaves and Weaving. ShuttleCraft Books, Coupeville, Washington.
The Techniques of Rug Weaving. Watson-Guptill Publications, New York 1968

Garrett, Cay
Warping All By Yourself. Interweave Press, Loveland, Colorado

Knutson, Linda
Shades of Wool for Kiton Dyes. Linda Knutson, Yakima, Washington 1986
Shades of Wool for Lanaset Dyes. Linda Knutson, Yakima, Washington 1983
Synthetic Dyes for Natural Fibers. Interweave Press, Loveland, Colorado

Kolander, Cheryl
A Silkworker's Notebook. Interweave Press, Loveland, Colorado, 1985

Kurtz, Carol S.
Designing for Weaving. Interweave Press, Loveland, Colorado, 1985

Lambert, Patricia, Staepelaere, Barbara and Fry, Mary G.
Color and Fiber. Schiffer Publishing, Ltd. West Chester, Pennsylvania, 1986

Mayer, Anita Luvera
Clothing from the Hands That Weave. Interweave Press, Loveland, Colorado, 1984
Handwoven Clothing, Felted to Wear. ShuttleCraft Books, Coupeville, Washington 1988

Moorman, Theo
Weaving as an Art Form. Schiffer Publishing, Ltd., West Chester, Pennsylvania

National Institute of Standards and Technology
Color: Universal Language and Dictionary of Names. Superintendent of Documents, U.S. Government Printing Office, Washington, D.C. 1976

Tidball, Harriet
ShuttleCraft Monographs, ShuttleCraft Books, Coupeville, Washington
Design and the Handweaver
Double Weave: Plain and Patterned
Peru: Textiles Unlimited
Peter Collingwood: His Weaves and Weaving
Surface Interest: Textiles of Today
Two-Harness Textiles, The Open Work Weaves

Vinroot, Sally and Crowder, Jennie
The New Dyer. Interweave Press, Loveland, Colorado, 1981

Appendix I Dyeing Glossary

Acetic acid. Chemical used as a dye assistant to fix dyes to protein fibers. Distilled white vinegar is 5% acetic, photographer's Glacial acetic is 56%. The dye bath for protein fibers should measure 4.0 to 4.5 acidity, measured with pH paper.

Acid Dye. Class of dyes used for protein fiber, which is fixed by the addition of acetic acid or other acid-forming compound.

All-purpose dye. Household or union dyes that contain chemicals that dye most fibers.

Batching. Fixing dyes with assistants by keeping them damp for a specified number of hours. Used for surface application of fiber reactive dyes.

Bleaching. Process of removing natural color from yarns.

Bleeding. Transfer of color from one area to another in washing.

Calgon. Commercial product which softens hard water; obtainable at supermarkets.

Cellulose fibers. Fibers based on vegetable products; includes rayon.

Chemical dyes. Chemically formulated dye; one type for protein fiber, others for cellulose fibers.

Color Index Numbers (C.I.) Numbers used in industry specifying colors in a particular dye series.

Colorfast. A color which does not fade when washed or exposed to light; resistance to fading is always relative.

Complementary Color. The color directly opposite another on the color wheel.

Crocking. Transfer of one color to another when dry, usually indicating that too much dye has been used or has not been properly fixed.

Depth of Shade (DOS). Amount of a given percent of stock solution required for a given amount of yarn in a given value; varies with different fibers and type of dye.

Dip Dyeing. Technique in which different parts of a skein are dipped in different colors; in acid dyes, the dye is often finished with a stop bath.

Direct Application. Application of dye without immersion in a bath, as in painting, printing, spraying.

Dye Assistants Chemicals used to keep the color level, or to fix the dye in the fiber

Dye Liquor Ratio. Relationship of the volume of water to the weight of fiber.

Dye lot. Fiber dyed in one dye run.

Dye run. Process of dyeing fiber all at once in one pot.

Exhaust. Transfer of dye to the fiber. In acid dyeing, if the bath is clear at the end of the dye run, it is said to be exhausted.

Fiber Reactive Dyes. Synthetic dyes for cellulose fibers and silk, often applied without heat.

Fixative. Chemical used to attach dye molecules to the fiber.

Float Skein. In acid dyeing, a small skein capped with plastic wrap which floats in the bath and can be removed during the dye run to check color or value.

Glacial acetic acid. An acid used in dyeing, which can be obtained at photography shops; strength usually used by dyers is 56%.

Glauber's salt. Salt used as a leveler which may improve exhaustion of color.

Graduate. A graduated cylinder used to measure liquids in milliliters or ounces, or both.

Gram. Unit of weight in the metric system. There are 28.351 grams to an ounce.

Household dye. All-purpose dyes obtainable in drug stores; same as union dyes.

Hue. A specific color, such as blue or green.

Hue gradation. A series of steps from one color to another in color mixing.

Hydrolysis. Characteristic of some dyes, particularly the fiber reactives, to color the bath rather than the fiber; must be allowed for in measuring the stock solutions.

Ikat. A method of forming patterns in yarns for woven textiles by tying the yarns tightly in predetermined places to resist the dye.

Dyeing Glossary (Continued)

Immersion dyeing. Placing the fiber in a dye bath which covers it, and heating or stirring with fixatives.

Kiton. Leveling acid dye for wool.

Leveler. Chemical included in a dye bath to slow the action of the dye for even results; in most cases a form of salt.

Leveling acid dye. Dye for protein fibers, requiring acid to fix the color and especially designed to level out during simmer; "Kiton" is one brand.

Liter. Metric unit of volume; 1000 milliliters contains 1 1/3 ounces more than a quart.

Milliliter (ml). One thousandth of a liter. A teaspoon contains 5 ml.

Natural dyes. Dyes derived from natural materials such as plants and minerals, many requiring chemicals in the form of mordants.

Overdyeing. Changing the color of a dyed fiber by re-dyeing it.

Percent of color. The percentage of each dyestock solution that makes up a mixed color.

Percent of shade. See Depth of shade.

pH paper. A form of litmus paper showing acidity or alkalinity of a liquid, using for comparison a color scale which is included with the package.

Pipette. Glass tube calibrated in ml for measuring small amounts of liquid. Obtainable from dye dealers or chemical supply houses.

Pre-metallized dye. A dye for protein fibers which has been formulated with metallic salts.

Primary color. A color that cannot be mixed from other colors. Primaries for dyeing are magenta, yellow and cyan blue (turquoise). Red and blue are also used as primaries to create a slightly different range of colors.

Processing. Techniques used to fix dye to the fibers.

Protein fibers. Fibers that come from animals, such as wool, hair and silk.

Rainbow dyeing. Processes used to dye yarn in two or more colors.

Residue. Color left in the bath after a dye run.

Resist. Term used to designate any substance which prevents dye from penetrating certain areas of fiber, such as ties or wax.

Scouring. Preparation of yarn for dyeing. In the case of cottons and linens, boiling in a laundry detergent. In the case of wool, silk and rayon, washing in soap or liquid detergent.

Secondary colors. Colors produced by mixing two of the primary colors - green, orange and purple.

Shade. Color resulting from mixing hues with color opposites or black.

Sizing. Finish applied to yarn or fabric to give it body; removed before dyeing.

Sodium acetate. Salt used for pre-metallized dyes.

Sodium alginate. Thickener for dyes for use in printing, spraying or painting to prevent blending of colors through wicking.

Sodium bicarbonate. Household soda referred to as "bicarb."

Sodium chloride. Ordinary table salt, used for leveling.

Sodium sulfate. Glauber's salt.

Stock solution. Liquid made from measured proportions of dye powders and water using syringes, graduates or pipettes.

Stop bath. A hot bath made of water and the dyeing amount of acid without dye, used to stop further darkening of color or, in the case of variegated dyes, blending of colors.

Strike. The point at which the color begins to appear on the fiber in the bath; varies with different colors even in the same series.

Stripping. Removal of color from the yarn or fiber.

Surface application. Applications of color to the fiber without immersion in a bath.

Synthetic fiber. Man-made fibers chemically produced: nylon, polyester and acrylic, et al.

Synthrapol. Liquid detergent, obtainable from dye dealers, useful for removing unfixed dye from fiber.

Syringe. Measuring device for liquids, usually calibrated in milliliters, which make it possible to measure small quantities. Obtainable at drug

Dyeing Glossary (Continued)

stores or pharmacy supply shops, sometimes by prescription only.

Tags. Short lengths of yarn attached to skeins before dyeing to sample effect of a given bath on yarns other than the skeins.

Tertiary colors. A hue obtained by mixing colors from three sides of the color wheel. May be three primaries, or a secondary and a primary opposite on the wheel.

Tie dyeing. A method in which some areas are tightly tied to prevent penetration of the dye.

Tint. A hue plus white. In the case of dyeing, this means using less dye than required for a full hue.

Tone. A light hue mixed with a color opposite or gray.

Unfixed dye. Dye that has not been attached to the fiber and remains in the bath or rinse.

Union dyes. Household or all-purpose dyes.

Value. Lightness or darkness of a color.

Value gradation. A set of samples of the same hue in steps from light to dark.

Variegated color. Two or more colors in one dye run using methods which do not blend them completely; "rainbow" dyeing.

Washing soda. Sodium carbonate. Washing soda from the laundry section of the supermarket may contain chemicals not suitable for dyeing.

Weight of fiber (WOF). Dry weight of fiber to be dyed.

Weight of goods (WOG). Same as weight of fiber.

Wetting out. Immersion of fiber in water before dyeing to help assure an even take up of the dye.

Appendix II
Table Of Equivalents For Dyers

WEIGHT

1 pound (lb)= 454 grams (g)

1 ounce (oz)= 28.35 g

LIQUID

1 milliliter (ml) water = 1 cubic centimeter (cc)

1 liter (l) = 1,000 ml = 1 quart + 54 ml

1 quart = 32 oz = 946 ml

1 pint = 16 oz = 473 ml

1 cup = 8 oz = 236 ml

1 ounce (oz) = 28.35 ml

1 tablespoon (tbs) = 1/2 oz = 15 ml

1 teaspoon (tsp) = 1/6 oz = 5 ml

Appendix III
Equipment And Supplies For Dyeing

EQUIPMENT

Important - Equipment used for dyeing should not be used for cooking.

Many of the items listed below are a one-time investment and will fit into a canner for storage.

All equipment should be stainless steel, glass, enamel or plastic

Quart jars for storing stock solutions and for hue and value gradations.

Pots: (enamel, glass, ceramic, stainless steel or Teflon - not iron or aluminum)

Canner with rack, for quantities of yarn over two ounces

Smaller pots for smaller amounts of yarn

Stainless or glass thermometer reading to 210^0

White ceramic or plastic cup

Measuring devices:

- Glass quart measure
- Set of stainless measuring cups (optional)
- Set of stainless steel measuring spoons
- Devices marked in milliliters:
- Graduates: 100 ml, or 600 ml, or both
- Plastic cups, marked in ounces and mls are quite accurate
- Baby bottles in 10 ml increments are also accurate
- Syringes: Choice of 1, 3, 5, 10 AND 30 ml (from drug store)

Pipettes, with bulbs, from your dye supplier

Spatula

Funnel

Heavily lined gloves, ample size, for handling hot yarns

Lightweight rubber gloves, not too big, or surgeon's gloves

Dust or mist masks

Small airtight jars to store dye powders

Timer

Scales: For weighing yarn, post office scales are fine for small amounts. If you can afford it, a triple beam balance weighs yarns up to 5.75 pounds and dye powders down to 1/10 gram. There is a less expensive balance (around $30) said to be quite accurate, obtainable from dye suppliers.

SUPPLIES

Dishwashing liquid such as Joy, Ivory or Palmolive (do not use Woolite)

Synthrapol detergent, obtainable from your dye dealer

Glacial acetic acid 56% (photography shop) or distilled white vinegar 5%

For fiber reactive dyes: washing soda (sodium carbonate) - do not use brand names from the laundry section of your supermarket

Sodium bicarbonate for some surface applications

Salt: uniodized table salt, or Glauber's salt

Paper Towels

Newspapers

Cotton string - cotton rug warp is best

pH paper from drug store, or short range pH paper from dye dealer

Saran or other plastic wrap that will withstand boiling water

SUPPLIERS

Cerulean Blue, Box 5126C, Seattle, WA 98105 (good catalog; much information)

Straw Into Gold, 5533 College Ave. Oakland, CA 95618

G & K Craft Industries (Prochem) PO Box 38, Somerset, MA 02726 - self- leveling acid dyes

Earth Guild, 1 Tingle Alley, Asheville, NC 28801

Dyekit, PO Box 1463, Mission, KS 66222

Appendix IV
Measuring Yarn For 5- and 10-gram Skeins

Ten-gram skeins are useful for making small samples of yarn in hue and value gradations. Directions are given below for this, and also directions for making 5-gram skeins for the very expensive silk.

When you buy yarn there is usually some indication of the number of yards to the pound, or in the case of knitting yarns, the number of grams to the skein. This is a figure you really need to know for dyeing. If you lack this information, use a reliable scale such as a postal scale. Wind a ball, and when it weighs one ounce, cut it off and measure the number of yards. Cut a piece of heavy cardboard to 18 inches and wind the yarn over it, each full turn measuring one yard. One-third of the number of turns will equal approximately 10 grams.

Silk is so expensive that a 7-step value or hue gradation using 10-gram skeins can cost several dollars. Five-gram skeins can be produced by dividing the number of yards per ounce by 6, for 1/6 ounce skeins, or approximately 5 grams.

There is a relatively inexpensive little gadget called the McMorran yarn balance. It consists of a plastic hook balanced over a plastic box. You place a length of yarn over the hook and start cutting off small snips until the hook is balanced. The length of yarn left on the hook is measured, and the number of inches multiplied by 100 gives you the number of yards to the pound. (There is also a metric version of the balance.) Tested against yarns of known yardage, the device proves to be quite accurate.

If you know the number of yards to the pound, it is easy to figure out the length of yarn necessary for 10 grams. In my primitive math, ten grams is yardage-per-pound divided by 16 for the number of yards to the ounce, divided by 3 for a third-ounce which is approximately 10 grams.

Further about silks: different silks take dyes differently so you can save both time and money by including several from your stock when making value and hue gradations. Another money-saver is to include tags of other silks when you are doing a full-scale dye run for a project.

Appendix V Self Leveling Acid Dyes (Kiton) on Wool

Stepped Reduction Of Values In One Hue, Canner Method

The process described below will produce samples of 10 grams (1/3 oz) each in a series of values of one hue, each sample being 50% lighter than its predecessor. It is planned for use with an ordinary canning kettle holding seven quart jars, and designed for beginning dyers as a first learning experience, since it avoids the problem of measuring very small amounts of stock solutions for the light values.

For information on measuring yarn for 10-gram skeins, see Appendix IV.

Starting with the darkest value, for example 2% depth of shade, the samples will run from strong to very pale. If you keep careful records it is easy to calculate the amount of stock solution for larger projects.

The process also provides small skeins in evenly graded values of a single hue, for embroiderers and tapestry weavers.

Equipment: Seven quart jars, numbered; canner with rack; syringes; graduates, cups

Yarn: Seven 10-gram skeins, dry weight (total 2 1/2 oz) wetted out and spun

Dye Assistants: Place the following in each jar:

Salt: 1/3 tsp, which is a rounded quarter-teaspoon

Vinegar: 10 mls

Stock Solution: Calculate the total of 1% stock solution on the weight of one 10-gram skein of yarn. Half of all the solution will be in Jar #1, and the rest distributed among the remaining six jars. Therefore, start with the amount of stock solution needed for the darkest value and **double** the amount. For example, 2 mls of stock will produce a dark value on 10 grams of yarn (2%). Doubled, this is 4 mls of stock.

Measuring Baths: Place all of the stock solution in a quart measure or graduate. Fill this with water to the 16-oz (2-cup) level. Mix well.

Pour one cup (8 oz) from the measure into Jar #1, which already contains salt and vinegar. This is 50% of the dye (20 mls or 2% depth of shade).

Refill the measure to the 16-oz mark, stir and pour one cup into Jar #2.

Refill the measure to the 16-oz mark, stir and pour one cup into Jar #3. Proceed in this manner through Jars 4, 5, and 6.

For the last jar, fill the graduate to 16 oz, pour one cup into jar #7 and discard the rest.

Processing: Add two cups of water to each jar, mix well, and stir into each a skein of yarn. Place jars in canner and surround them with water to the level of the dye. Heat the canner to a boil, stirring the yarn frequently. When the temperature in the jars reaches 180^0 to 200^0, start timing and hold at this temperature for 45 minutes, stirring frequently.

Turn off the heat and allow the yarn to cool in the jars. Residues in the bath will be nearly clear. Rinse, wash with liquid detergent and dry.

Tag each skein with a note as to the proportions of 1% stock solution to the weight of yarn - this is the "depth of shade". In the lighter values, the color may not be completely level, but the shading will be quite accurate.

If larger samples are wanted, the amounts of yarn, dye assistants and stock solutions can be doubled, but the results may not be completely level.

Value gradations are particularly valuable in secondary and tertiary colors, because in the lighter values, the color mixtures are more evident than in the darker shades.

Appendix VI Self-leveling Acid Dyes (Kiton) on Wool

Hue Gradations In Two Or More Colors, Canner Method

The process described below will produce samples of 10 grams (1/3 oz) each, in a series of mixtures of two hues. An ordinary canning kettle will hold seven quart jars; if you have a nine quart canner, the number of steps can be increased to nine.

For information on measuring yarn for 10-gram skeins, see Appendix IV.

By recording the amount and proportion of each color in each sample, you will find it easy to calculate the quantity and mixture of stock solutions needed for larger projects. Each sample will be at 1% depth of shade.

The process also provides small skeins of graded hues for embroiderers and tapestry weavers.

Equipment: Seven numbered quart jars, canner with rack, syringes, graduates, cups

Yarn: Seven 10 g skeins (total about 2 1/2 oz) dry weight

Stock Solutions: For medium depth of shade, 10 total mls of 1% stock solution to each jar.

Dye Assistants: Salt, 1/3 tsp each jar (rounded quarter teaspoons)

Vinegar, 10 mls each jar

Preparing Baths: Number quart jars, and label each with the amount of diluted stock solution of each color needed (see table below). Place in each jar slightly less than three cups of water. To each jar add 10 mls of vinegar and a rounded quarter-teaspoon of salt. Add diluted stock solutions prepared according the instructions below, in the amounts shown in the table under the heading "Diluting Stock Solutions."

Diluting Stock Solutions: Some of the stock solutions are used in such small quantities that it is difficult to measure them accurately. I suggest, therefore, that you dilute them for ease in measuring. Place 35 mls of each stock solution in two separate containers, and add enough water to each to bring the liquid up to 140 mls, four times the amount of stock solution.

Using syringes, measure the diluted solutions into the labeled jars according to the table below.

Processing: Stir jars well, add one wetted-out skein of wool to each, and place on the rack in the canner. Surround the jars with water to the level of the dye. Cover, and raise the water in the canner to a boil, stirring the yarn frequently. When the temperature in the jars reaches 180^0, start timing. Hold at that temperature for 45 minutes, stirring at intervals. Let the yarn stand in the baths while cooling to room temperature.

Remove skeins one by one, labeling as you go with masking tape and ballpoint pen, showing the number of the jar for future notes. Wash and dry.

Colors will be quite level, and the residue in the baths nearly clear.

Notes: For tertiary colors, use one primary and one secondary, or three colors from three sides of the color wheel. Keep careful notes! For example: orange consisting of one part red to seven parts yellow, plus blue, will produce shading from grayed blue through brown to grayed orange. Purple plus yellow in a hue gradation will produce grayed purple through brown to grayed yellow, and red plus green will produce grayed red through brown to grayed green.

Application of this method to variegated color: If "Rainbow" colors are wanted, the salt could be omitted and the stock solutions separately added after the yarns have been heated in the jars. Do not stir.

Or non-leveling dyes such as Lanaset/Telana could be used, without salt or stirring.

The "stuffed pot" method could also be used, which involves placing more than 10 grams of yarn in each jar and increasing the stock solutions proportionately, then processing without stirring.

Sample #	Color Proportions (%)			Stock Solutions (ml)*		Diluted Stock Solutions (ml)**	
	Color A		Color B	Color A	Color B	Color A	Color B
(1)	7	to	1	8.75	1.25	35	05
(2)	6	to	2	7.5	2.5	30	10
(3)	5	to	3	6.25	3.75	25	15
(4)	4	to	4	5.0	5.0	20	20
(5)	3	to	5	3.75	6.25	15	25
(6)	2	to	6	2.5	7.25	10	30
(7)	1	to	7	1.25	8.75	05	35

* Use these figures for labeling samples

**Use these figures for jar labels

Appendix VII Level Dyeing with Cibacron F - Cellulose, Silk And Wool

Bear in mind that different silks will take dye differently and it is necessary to test them before undertaking a large dye run.

Yarn Preparation: Cellulose fibers may need to be scoured by boiling in water with detergent for 15 to 30 minutes to remove natural waxes or chemicals applied during spinning. Mercerized cottons, rayons and silks require only washing.

Stock Solutions: These are usually used in the amount of 2% or more of the weight of fiber, but because the stock solutions have a relatively short life, it makes more sense to prepare them at 1% and double the amount for a 2% depth of shade. This means 10 grams of dye powder to 1000 grams of water. (A teaspoon of powder weighs about two grams, so the teaspoon measurement would be five level teaspoons to a quart of water.) Using hot water, measure out the total amount needed. Add a little to the dye powder and mix it to a paste. Add the rest of the water and stir until no lumps or grains are visible, add one drop of vinegar. Label with color, type of dye, and date. Store in a dark place.*

The black dye is relatively weak and brownish; for a real black you must use about 10 times the amount of stock solution you need for the other colors.

Cellulose and Silk with Sodium Carbonate (Washing Soda) Fixative

Processing: Make a mixture of hot water (140^0) in the amount of 30 times the weight of the fiber, salt calculated on the weight of the fiber (75 to 100%) and the amount of stock solution you need for the depth of shade you plan.

Mix well to dissolve the salt. Add the wetted-out fiber and stir frequently for 30 minutes. If you cover the dyepot between stirs, the temperature will stay up during the run.

Measure washing soda in the amount of 30% of the weight of fiber, and add just enough hot water to dissolve it. Remove the yarn from the bath, stir in the soda solution, return the yarn and stir frequently for 45 minutes.

Finishing: Rinse the fiber with much water, first in cold, then in hot, until little color can be seen in the run-off water. Then put the yarn in a pot on the heat source and add Synthrapol or other detergent. Simmer for 10 minutes. Rinse in several short hot baths until the water is entirely clear. Do not heat silk above 170^0.

You can check the presence of loose dye by pressing a strand of wet yarn with an iron, between two layers of white cloth.

Silk and Wool with Vinegar as Fixative

This method is not much mentioned in the texts, but I find it easier to use than the soda method, probably because of a misspent youth using leveling acid dyes. It will not work with cellulose fibers, which require soda.

Please note: the vinegar approach works well with silk, which dyes with a temperature as low as 125^0, but the temperature for wool must be around 180^0 to fix the color. Silk dyes beautifully to 175^0, and in the same bath wool takes a much darker value than the silk.

Yarn preparation is the same as for the soda fixative.

Processing: Place dye and salt in a stainless pot on a heat source. When the salt is dissolved, add the yarn. Raise the temperature to 175^0, remove the yarn and add vinegar in the amount of an ounce of vinegar to an ounce of yarn. Stir well, and return the yarn to the bath. Keep the temperature close to 175^0, stirring gently at intervals. (Wool can take up to 200^0, but not silk.) Allow the yarn to cool in the bath to room temperature. Rinse, wash and rinse again. In the case of silk, use vinegar in the last rinse in the amount of 1% of the weight of the fiber, and allow to stand for a few minutes.

This method is offered for several reasons. My experiments show that the color is usually completely level, and the color is stronger than with soda as fixative, which means there is less dye to be rinsed out. Additionally, the method adapts well to experiments such as hue and value gradations on wool and silk, and painted-and-steamed and casserole methods.

Again about silks: You may find some differences in hue between silks dyed with soda and identical baths using vinegar. For example, samples using the same weight of yarn and the same amount of dye but one using vinegar and the other soda had this curious result: the soda bath produced silk that was substantially lighter and definitely more pink; the vinegar bath with the same dye content (half magenta, half blue) produced true purples and was much darker. Since silk is very expensive, this means a cautious approach with careful sampling. You will save trouble and expense if you make a practice of including tags of other silks in every bath you dye.

* Cibacron F will keep its strength longer if stored in the refrigerator, and even longer in a freezer.

Appendix VIII Value Gradations In One Hue, Cibacron F – Cellulose, Silk & Wool

One of the most useful tools to have in your dye workshop is a set of samples of value gradations (light to dark) for each dye color in your stock, plus mixtures.

The process described below will produce samples of five grams (1/6 ounce) each in a series of values of one hue, each sample being 50% lighter than its predecessor. It is planned for use with an ordinary canning kettle, with rack holding seven quart jars, and designed for beginning dyers as a first learning experience, since it avoids the problem of measuring very small amounts of stock solution for the lighter values.

For information on measuring yarn for 5- and 10-gram skeins, see Appendix IV.

Starting with the darkest value, for example 4% depth of shade, the samples will run from deep to very pale. If you keep careful records, it is easy to calculate the amount of stock solution for larger projects.

The process also provides small skeins in evenly graded values of a single hue, for embroiderers and tapestry weavers.

Cibacron F on Silk and Wool with Vinegar Fixative

Equipment: Seven quart jars, numbered; canner with rack; syringes; graduates; cups

Yarn: Seven 5-gram skeins, dry weight (total about 1 1/4 oz.); wetted out and spun

Dye Assistants: salt, vinegar

Stock solution: Calculate the total of 1% stock solution on the weight on one 5-gram skein of yarn. Half of all the solution will be in Jar #1, and the rest distributed among the remaining six jars. Therefore, start with the amount of stock solution needed for the darkest value and double the amount. For example, 20 ml of 1% stock solution will produce a deep value on five grams of yarn; doubled, this is 40 ml of stock for the entire dye run. The depth of shade will start at 4% in Jar #1, and the values in subsequent jars will be 2%, 1%, .5%, .25%, .125%,. and .0625%. If you multiply the weight of yarn in a project by one of these percentages, you will know how many milliliters of dye to use.

Measuring baths; Place all of the stock solution in a quart measure or graduate. Add 200 ml of water, mix well. Pour 100 ml of the mixture into Jar #1. Add 100 ml of water to the remainder, mix well, and pour 100 ml into Jar #2. Proceed in this manner until you reach the last jar - after the addition of 100 ml of water, mix well and pour 100 ml of the mixture into the last jar. DISCARD THE REST.

Add to each jar 3/4 tsp salt, 5 ml vinegar, and 50 ml water, bringing the dye- liquor ratio to 30:1 (weight of fiber times 30).

Place the jars on the rack in the canner, add a skein of yarn to each, mix well. Add water around the jars to the level of the dye. Raise the temperature slowly until it measures 175 in the jars, stirring gently at intervals. Hold the temperature at 175 for 45 minutes. The water in the jars will slowly evaporate; add small amounts of boiling water now and then to keep the baths at the original level.

After 45 minutes, cool yarn in baths. Wash in cold, then hot water with detergent or Synthrapol. Rinse until clear. Add a tablespoon of vinegar to a quart of water for the next to last rinse.

Silks dyed in this manner will retain their luster and the color will be much deeper than methods using soda or vinegar without heat.

Wools can be dyed with Cibacron F by this method, and the values will be stronger than those on silk. The temperature should be allowed to rise to 180 to 200.

Cibacron F on Silk and Cellulose with Soda Fixative

Equipment: Seven jars, numbered, pan for hot water, syringes, graduates, cups

Yarn: Seven 5-gram skeins, dry weight (total about 1 1/4 ounces) wetted out.

Dye Assistants: Salt, washing soda (Sodium Carbonate)

Stock Solutions: Calculate these the same way as given under "Silk and Wool with Vinegar Fixative," above.

Measuring Bath: Place all the stock solution in a graduate or cup. Add 200 ml of water and stir well. Pour 100 ml of mixture into Container #1. Add 100 ml of water to the remainder, mix well and pour 100 ml of mixture into container #2. Proceed in this manner until you reach the last jar. For this, add 100 ml of water to the graduate, pour into 100 ml into the last jar, and DISCARD THE REST.

Add 50 ml of water to each jar, bringing the dye/liquor ratio to 30:1, or a total of 150 ml for five g of yarn.

Add 3/4 tsp salt to each container, and dissolve. Add one 5-g skein of yarn.

Place all jars in a pan of hot water and cover, to keep the temperature of the bath at 140^0 or under. Stir at frequent intervals for 30 minutes.

Remove skeins and add to each container 1.5 g (1/2 tsp) of washing soda, dissolved in a minimum of hot water. (For seven containers this would be 10.5 g or 5 1/4 tsp of soda. You could use a measured amount of hot water and divide the liquid evenly among the jars.) Return the yarn to the baths.

Stir frequently for 45 minutes.

Finish as described under directions for vinegar fixative.

Appendix IX Hue Gradations, Cibacron F – Cellulose, Silk & Wool

Hue gradations are an important tool for dyers. They consist of a series of mixtures of two or more primaries on a graded scale, and they will help you find the two- and three-color combinations you need. Don't overlook the browns and grays you will find in mixing color opposites (purple-yellow, red-green, blue-orange.)

When you mix the primaries magenta and turquoise, you may get some surprises.

The process described below will produce samples of five grams (1/6 oz) each, in a series of mixtures of two hues. An ordinary canning kettle will hold seven quart jars; if you have a 9-quart canner the number of steps can be increased to nine.

For information on measuring yarn for 5- and 10-gram skeins, see Appendix IV.

By recording the amount and proportion of each color in each sample, you will be able to calculate the quantity and color mixture of stock solutions for larger projects. The following directions will be at 1% depth of shade, which is regarded as medium in fiber reactive dyes.

Cibacron F on Silk and Wool with Vinegar Fixative

Equipment: Seven numbered quart jars, canner with rack, syringes, graduates,

Yarn: Seven 5-gram skeins, dry weight (total about 1 1/4 oz) wetted out.

Stock solutions: For 1% depth of shade, five ml (total of all colors) of 1% stock solution in each jar.

Dye assistants: salt, vinegar.

Preparing baths: Label each jar with the amount of diluted stock solution of each color needed (see table below).

Diluting stock solutions: Some of the stock solutions are used in such small amounts that it is difficult to measure them accurately, so it is suggested that you dilute them for ease in measuring.

Place 35 ml of each stock solution in separate containers, one for each color. Add enough water to each to bring the liquid up to 140 ml.

Using syringes, measure the diluted solutions into the numbered and labeled jars according to the table below.

Sample #	Color Proportions (%)			Stock Solutions (ml)*		Diluted Stock Solutions (ml)**	
	Color A		Color B	Color A	Color B	Color A	Color B
(1)	7	to	1	4.375	0.625	35	05
(2)	6	to	2	3.750	1.250	30	10
(3)	5	to	3	3.125	1.875	25	15
(4)	4	to	4	2.500	2.500	20	20
(5)	3	to	5	1.875	3.125	15	25
(6)	2	to	6	1.250	3.750	10	30
(7)	1	to	7	0.625	4.375	05	35

* Use these figures for labeling samples

**Use these figures for jar labels

Appendix IX (Continued)

Each jar now contains 5 ml dye, 35 ml water, total 40 ml.

Add to each jar 3/4 tsp of salt, 5 ml vinegar.

Add wetted-out yarn, one skein to each jar, stir well, and place the jar on the rack in the canner. Surround the jars with water to the level of the dye.

Cover the canner, and raise the water in the canner to a boil, stirring yarn frequently. When the temperature in the jars reaches 175 degrees, start timing. Hold at this temperature for 45 minutes, stirring at intervals. Remove jars and let the yarn stand in the bath while cooling to room temperature.

Remove skeins one by one, labeling as you go with masking tape and ballpoint pen, showing the number of the jar for future notes. Wash and dry. Rinse in cold water, then wash in hot water with dishwashing detergent or Synthrapol. Rinse until clear.

For tertiary colors, use one primary and one secondary color. Keep careful notes. For example, if Color A is purple, (half magenta, half blue) and Color B is yellow, you will get hues from grayed purple through brown to golds.

The same system will dye 5-gram samples of wool, in much darker values. It would pay you to include a small tag of wool with silk samples, and vice versa.

Cibacron F on Cellulose and Silk with Soda Fixative

Equipment: **Seven numbered quart jars or small containers, syringes, graduates**

Yarn: Seven 5-gram skeins (total 1 1/4 oz) dry weight, wetted out

Stock Solutions: for 1% depth of shade, five ml (total of all color) of 1% stock solution for each container.

Dye Assistants: salt, washing soda

Preparing Baths: Label each jar with the amount of diluted stock solution of each color needed according to the table in the section above on hue gradations using a vinegar fixative.

Diluted Stock Solutions: refer to the explanation in the section on hue gradations using vinegar fixative, above.

When the stock solutions have been placed in the containers, each now contains 5 ml of dye, 35 ml of water, totaling 40 ml. Add to each jar 110 ml of hot water.

Add to each jar 3/4 tsp of salt, and stir to dissolve.

Add wetted-out yarn, one skein to each container, stir well. Place in a pan of hot water. Cover to maintain temperature of about 140^0 in the containers.

Stir yarn frequently for 30 minutes.

Remove skeins and add to each container 1.5 g (1/2 tsp) of washing soda, dissolved in a minimum of hot water. (For seven containers, this would be 10.5 g for 5 1/4 tsp of soda. You could use a measured amount of hot water and divide the liquid evenly among the containers.)

Stir frequently for 45 minutes.

Remove skeins one by one, labeling with masking tape and ballpoint pen as you go, noting the number of the jar for future reference. Rinse in cold water, then hot. Wash in hot water with detergent or Synthrapol. Rinse until clear.

For tertiary colors, use one primary and one secondary.

Appendix X Sampling For Hue and Value, and Variegated Colors, On Single Skeins

CIBACRON F, PROCION LIQUID H AND PROCION MX

Single skeins are painted with the stock solutions (as described below). This method is quicker than stepped reductions in jars, but it is apt to be less accurate, depending on the care you use in measuring and recording the stock solutions.

Painting silk and wool with vinegar fixative: The stock solutions are prepared in small containers, noting the mixtures of colors or the dilution of values. A single skein is wetted out in a solution of 1 tbs vinegar to a quart of water, and allowed to stand for an hour, then squeezed and laid out on plastic wrap. Using paintbrushes, syringes or foam brushes, the dye is applied in bands across the skein, with white space left between the bands to avoid mixing the colors or values, Roll the pastic wrap loosely around the yarn and snake it around a rack in a canning kettle, with boiling water underneath. Steam wool for 20 minutes, silk for 15 minutes. Rinse and wash. Very heavy skeins may require more time for thorough heating.

Painting cellulose and silk with soda fixative: Skeins are wetted out with a soda solution (dissolve 2 tbs washing soda in 250 mls hot water) and allowed to stand for a half hour, then spun or squeezed. Stock solution is applied with syringes or brushes, leaving white spaces between colors. Skeins are then wrapped or covered airtight and allowed to stand for 24 to 48 hours. (This is called "batching.")

For liquid Procion H, the dye is allowed to dry completely and the skeins are then put in the dryer at high heat for 30 minutes.

Variegated or Rainbow Dyeing

Paint with stock solutions as described above, but encourage the colors to overlap or blend, and check to be sure there are no white areas underneath. Stock solutions may be applied lengthwise, with colors side by side.

Casserole Dyeing on Silk and Wool with Vinegar Solution: This is possible only for silk and wool, but it produces very strong color with little wash-off. Wet the yarn out in a solution of 1 tbs of vinegar to a quart of water, drain and apply the stock solutions with syringes or squeeze bottles. Cover and place in a preheated oven at 300^0 for 15 minutes. Add hot water (175^0) and heat 30 minutes.

Appendix XI Inkodye on Cellulose & Silk

Inkodye is somewhat of a nuisance to use on large amounts of yarn because it must be exposed to sunlight, and involves a lot of stirring and tossing during development of the color. It will dye cotton and silk, and is particularly successful on rayon.

Inkodyes come in bottles, and the liquids are gray to colorless, so it is necessary to sample each dye bath. This is done simply by soaking a short length of yarn in dye and exposing it to the sun. Inkodye is much easier to use than the fiber reactives for some of the more free-wheeling techniques, since all that is required is water.

It does not come in a complete color range – Cerulean Blue stocks it in red, red-orange, yellow, blue-green, blue, red-violet, brown and black. The dye labeled brown is really quite gray and is valuable as a toner. The black is purplish, which makes it hard to dye a range of true grays, though the addition of yellow would help. All the color mix together beautifully and give soft to brilliant colors.

The colors seem to be extremely fast – in fact impossible to remove with Clorox, so be careful of your clothing and your white Formica counters. (You won't know you have spilled them until the colors appear, at which point it is too late.) The company recommends keeping the dye for only two years, but I am using some colors I acquired 15 years ago.

Safety: Outdoor use is recommended, or indoors with an ammonia vapor filter in a respirator. I do not find it strongly ammoniac, so I choose to ignore this. My dyeing, however, is done in a room with a 12-foot ceiling.

Cottons and linens should be scoured by simmering 20 minutes in laundry detergent, and thoroughly rinsed. Rayon and silk need only be washed. For the procedure below, all yarns should be dried after scouring.

Dye Baths: Colors can be diluted with plain water. A mixture of one part dye to five parts water on yarn produces a very strong value, 1 to 10 is medium, and 1 to 20 or 30 and up, nice pastels. For accuracy, use syringes for the stock solution and graduates for the water, both in milliliters. Dip a test length of wetted-out yarn in the bath you plan to use, and expose to sunlight.

Skeining: Use small skeins, 1 oz or less for fine yarns because they are easier to expose to the sun. Use the following ties:

A long interwoven tie in a colored string where the skein ends meet - this to be left in the skein for the entire process.

Seven short ties, quite loose, in another color, to be removed when the yarn is spread over a dowel during development of the color, and restored before removing from the dowel for washing.

Process: Wear gloves. Wet out the skein for several hours in a measured amount of water to barely cover. After wetting out, squeeze the water from the yarn into a container, and use this to mix the dye. Base your dye proportion on the amount of water used to wet out the yarn. Place the wet yarn into the bath and stir, out of the sunlight, for 15 minutes, occasionally squeezing the skein as you stir.

Squeeze the dye from the yarn (saving the bath) and hang the skein over a dowel in the sun. Remove the short ties and spread out over the dowel. If it is a sunny, breezy day, a minimum of handling is necessary - shake the skeins and rotate them around the dowel so that all areas are exposed to light.

Be patient. Some colors appear instantly to surprise you, but blues go through several shades of gray before reaching their true color. If allowed to stand overnight and exposed again the next day, the color will gradually level. They can be developed slowly in a sunny window or outdoors on a cloudy day. Restore the short ties, wash, rinse and dry.

SAVE ALL BATHS. There will be lots of bath left over. If kept in total darkness they will dye yarns in lighter shades for a long time, or leftovers can be mixed for blended hues. "Second-hand" baths will be lighter than the original. If a stored bath shows much color, test it before using.

The dye contains ammonia, but when diluted shows a pH of "weakly basic," which is not very intimidating. Silks should be treated with vinegar in the next to last rinse.

For variegated colors, it is fun to improvise - dip wet skeins in several colors; lay a skein in the sun and pour the dye over it; hang the skein and spray with colors; stretch a warp and paint it; print with sponges; use ikat ties. You can think up other methods.

The dye will work on dry yarn, which means that it would be possible to use it to paint a warp tensioned on the loom. However, it is fairly difficult to get the dye to penetrate, and the color develops very slowly in a room, even with a skylight, a matter of days.

The quickest results would be obtained if you could put the loom outdoors in the sun, or you could tension the warp on a frame which could be placed outside. The ideas don't seem to be very practical, but perhaps my attitude is affected by the fact that I don't much care for warps painted on the loom because the colors are sometimes diluted by the color of the weft.

Hue and value gradations can easily be made by dunking very small wetted-out skeins in successive mixtures of color combinations and of dye mixed with water.

Appendix XII

PROJECT ______________________________

Date __________ Dye ______________________________

FIBERS	WEIGHT	SOURCE
__________	________	__________________
__________	________	__________________
__________	________	__________________
__________	________	__________________
__________	________	__________________
Total Weight	________	

STOCK SOLUTIONS (%) COLOR DESCRIPTION:

color #1 ________ ml

color #2 ________ ml DEPTH OF SHADE ______ %

color #3 ________ ml

Total ________ ml

BATH	ACID DYE	FIBER REACTIVE DYE
Water	____________	____________
Salt/Leveler	____________	____________
Stock solutions, total	____________	____________
Fixative	____________	____________

PROCESSING:

NOTES AND COMMENTS:

Level? ____ Residue ____ Washoff ____ Shrinkage_____%

REFERENCES:

FOLD HERE

SAMPLES

Original Colors

Wet-matching?

Finished Color

TAGS:

Appendix XIII

YARNS: Description Source YARDAGE: Official Actual Dyed YARN SAMPLES

Warps:

Wefts:

WARP LENGTH CALCULATION

(Estimated take-up/Shrinkage ______ %)

List each piece	Inches needed
____________________	______________
____________________	______________
____________________	______________
____________________	______________
____________________	______________
____________________	______________
Total finished length	______________

ALLOWANCES:

Take-up, shrinkage	______________
Tie-ins, thrums	______________
Cut-offs (5" each)	______________
Samples	______________
TOTAL INCHES	______________
TOTAL YARDS	______________

YARN REQUIREMENT CALCULATION

(Estimated take-up/Shrinkage ______ %)

Reed ______ Sley______ EPI ______

WARP REQUIRED

# of ends in warp	______________
x total length	______________
Yards in warp	______________
Actual length of warp chains	______________
Weight of warp chains	______________

WEFT REQUIRED

# of inches/pick	______________
x # of picks/inch	______________
x # yds/woven inch	______________
x # inches woven	______________
= TOTAL YARN IN YARDS	______________

WOVEN MEASUREMENTS

	On loom, tensioned	Off loom	Fulled	Take-up, shrinkage
Width	________	________	________	________
Length	________	________	________	________

Weight of finished piece __________

WEFT RECORD

Weft at start	________
- Weft left	________
TOTAL USED	________

Finishing notes, comments: (Attach drafts, sketches, samiples, snapshots, warp layout)

INDEX